Experiencing Prayer

with Jesus

EXPERIENCING PRAYER *with*
JESUS

HENRY & NORMAN
BLACKABY

Multnomah® Publishers *Sisters, Oregon*

EXPERIENCING PRAYER WITH JESUS
published by Multnomah Publishers, Inc.

© 2006 by Henry T. Blackaby and Norman C. Blackaby
International Standard Book Number: 1-59052-576-0

Cover design by The DesignWorks Group, Inc.
Front cover image by Guildhall Art Gallery,
Corporation of London Bridgeman Art Library, London/Superstock
Back cover image by Tom Stewart/Corbis

Italics in Scripture quotations are the authors' emphasis.
Unless otherwise indicated, Scripture quotations are from:
The Holy Bible, New King James Version © 1984 by Thomas Nelson, Inc.
Other Scripture quotations are from:
The Amplified Bible (AMP)
© 1965, 1987 by Zondervan Publishing House.
The Amplified New Testament © 1958, 1987 by the Lockman Foundation.
The Holy Bible, New International Version (NIV)
© 1973, 1984 by International Bible Society,
used by permission of Zondervan Publishing House
The Holy Bible, *English Standard Version* (ESV)
© 2001 by Crossway Bibles, a division of Good News Publishers.
Used by permission. All rights reserved.

Multnomah is a trademark of Multnomah Publishers, Inc., and is registered in the U.S. Patent and
Trademark Office. The colophon is a trademark of Multnomah Publishers, Inc.

Printed in the United States of America

For information:
MULTNOMAH PUBLISHERS, INC. • 601 N. LARCH ST. • SISTERS, OR 97759
ISBN 978-1-59052-576-0

CONTENTS

FOR A LIFE-CHANGING ENCOUNTER WITH CHRIST

We have opportunity in our ministry to interact with numerous people through conferences, online discipleship classes, Bible study groups, Sunday services, and meetings with business leaders. We encounter so many wonderful believers who have an earnest desire to live a life pleasing to God and effective in His kingdom. Very often they express to us a deep burden to understand and grow particularly in the area of prayer.

These Christians enjoy reading their Bible, serving in their local church or ministry, and sharing their faith, but again and again they tell us that they don't see victory in their prayer life. Even when they spend considerable time in prayer, they often fail to sense that their prayers are vital or effective.

As we've heard these longings from God's people, God has placed a burden on our hearts to write this book.

In doing so, our goals are these:

1. To open afresh your mind and heart to the prayer life of Jesus.

2. To help you anticipate and recognize the activity of God in your prayer life as He conforms you to the image of His Son.

3. To exhort you to obey and respond to all of the fullness of God—Father, Son, and Holy Spirit—as He develops your prayer life.

4. To help you see the immediate urgency of the hour in which we live, and the impact we can have through our prayers.

5. To show that immediate and thorough obedience is key to your prayer life.

LOOK TO GOD'S ENABLING

Our desire is that *Experiencing Prayer with Jesus* will not be simply more information about prayer for you, but that it will lead you to a life-changing encounter with Christ...and therefore forever rearrange your prayer life into continuing fellowship with our Lord.

While there are many wonderful examples of prayer

and passages on prayer throughout the Scriptures, we know of no better model and demonstration of what the heavenly Father desires for our prayer life than the life of our Lord Jesus Christ. And at this critical time in history, we don't need simply "more prayer" from God's people; we need specifically the kind of praying exemplified in the life of Christ. Therefore we'll be focusing especially in these pages on closely observing our Savior in prayer.

In any such study, it becomes immediately evident that there's a significant difference between how Jesus prayed and the prayer life of many Christians today. Recognizing this gap, it's easy to feel that His heart of prayer and the dynamic characteristics of His prayer life are things that will never become a part of our own experience.

However, as you become more aware of this gap in your own life, we urge you *not to become discouraged.* Instead, press ahead to ask, *"Why* is there this difference?" and especially, "How can I allow the Holy Spirit to change my prayer life to be more like the Lord's?"

He Himself often withdrew into the wilderness and prayed.

LUKE 5:16

Be assured that God not only desires that we pray in a Christlike manner, but He also *enables* us to do so. Through His Holy Spirit within us, the Father is working to conform us "to the image of His Son" (Romans 8:29; see also Galatians 2:20), and this transformation will preeminently involve and affect our prayer life.

FOR BEING USED BY GOD

When we look at the people God used in the Scriptures as well as those He used throughout Christian history, we see their lives marked by a deep awareness and practice of prayer with their heavenly Father. In most of the biographies and testimonies from people whom God has used in mighty ways in the past, there's a confession that the key to their work and to the measure in which it honored God is directly linked to prayer that mirrored the prayer experience of Jesus.

We believe this link is needed today as much as ever. There's an urgent necessity for the requests and supplications of God's people to reflect the prayer life of Jesus Christ as we see it unfolded in the Scriptures.

From Henry: Now It's Our Turn

Probably no Scripture in recent years has affected me as much as the last verses of Hebrews chapter eleven. Having given us earlier in this chapter a whole catalogue of the great men and women of faith, the chapter concludes, "And all these, having obtained a good testimony through faith, did not receive the promise, God having provided something better for us, *that they should not be made perfect apart from us"* (Hebrews 11:39–40).

There are those who have gone before—and now it's *our* turn. There are those who have carried the torch, who have prayed through the night and wept through the night, praying for revival in our land. However, they did not see what God promised—and now it's up to us. If we don't continue the vigil to pray, we delay even more the completion of what was begun by those who've gone before us.

I've often said to the Lord, "O God, many others have begun and never saw the completion of your promises in their generation. O Lord, help me to be faithful *in my generation* that when I pray, I hear from You…and that when I hear from You, I immediately adjust my life accordingly."

Chapter One

OUR KEY TO LIFE AND MINISTRY

The twelve disciples whom Jesus chose were no doubt men who prayed. They had been raised in a culture that valued and practiced prayer, and each of their hearts must have been prayerfully tender toward God for each man to leave everything and follow after Jesus when He extended His call to them.

And yet, as the disciples went on to closely observe Jesus, they consistently noticed a stark difference between their way of praying and the prayer life of the Lord.

In the presence of these twelve men, Jesus both taught and modeled a radical life of prayer, and it caught their attention. We see this, for example, in Luke 11:1. Jesus "was praying in a certain place," and when He finished, "one of His disciples said to Him, 'Lord, teach us to pray.'" They wanted something better than they already had; they wanted the same reality and vitality of prayer that Jesus experienced.

So He taught them. And everything He taught, He also lived out before them.

AT THE CENTER OF HIS LIFE

Jesus urged these disciples to always pray and never lose heart (Luke 18:1), to "cry out day and night" to God (18:7), and to keep asking and seeking and knocking with confident assurance of the Father's loving heart (Matthew 7:7–11). Hearing Jesus say these things, the Twelve could not forget that even while He ministered to "great multitudes" through continual preaching and healing, "He Himself often withdrew into the wilderness and prayed" (Luke 5:16). They had witnessed how the Lord rose "a long while before daylight" and "went out and departed to a solitary place; and there He prayed" (Mark 1:35). They knew their Master as One who "went out to the mountain to pray, and continued all night in prayer to God" (Luke 6:12).

The conclusion was inescapable: Jesus' prayer life was the key to both His life and ministry.

Throughout the scriptural record of the ministry of our Lord, it's clear that prayer is one of the most marked characteristics of His life. At each major juncture, at every key decision point, we find Him in prayer.

It was true in the very beginning: At the time of His baptism, it was "while He prayed" that "heaven was opened" and the Holy Spirit came down upon Him like a dove while the Father audibly assured Him, "You are My beloved Son; in You I am well pleased" (Luke 3:21–22).

And it was true as well at the end, as Jesus continued praying on the cross (Matthew 27:46; Luke 23:34,46).

Every part of our Lord's life was centered and guided by His continuing communication with the Father.

And when He had sent the multitudes away,
He went up on the mountain
by Himself to pray.
Now when evening came,
He was alone there.

MATTHEW 14:23

From Norman: **Early Morning Habit**

Watching my parents over the years, I would definitely characterize them as people of prayer. If you asked any of the five children in our family what our dad was doing in the early morning hours, each one would answer, "He's praying and studying his Bible."

To this day when I visit their home, I know that no matter how early I get up in the morning, my father will already be in prayer and the Scriptures in his office.

One night last year our daughter became very ill. Some time after midnight we decided to take her to the hospital, where it was determined that she needed to have an IV put in. Our daughter is very afraid of needles and we knew this would scare her. We immediately wanted to telephone Mom and Dad and ask for their prayers.

By then it was about three o'clock in the morning, and about five o'clock where my parents live. We called them— and they were already awake and ready to pray, just as I expected.

It was such a comfort to me to know I could call at such an early hour and know they would be praying as we walked through a difficult sickness with our daughter.

So often, as we read about Jesus, we fail to make the connection between His example and our own experience. From God's perspective, however, the characteristics of His Son's prayer life are to be true for every believer and every church.

We easily dismiss that fact. We tell ourselves, "Jesus was the Son of God; of course His prayer life was outstanding. But I'm only human; I can't be expected to pray as Christ prayed."

There are plenty of Scriptures to counter that argument, and one of them is a profound passage we'll refer to often in this book as we explore it phrase by phrase. For catching the heart of Christ's prayer life in relation to the Father, we know of no passage better than Hebrews 5:7–9, which describes the intense manner and momentous results of the prayers Jesus offered. These verses pull together the entire prayer life of Jesus into a single, powerful statement for our instruction. It teaches us the essence of prayer, so we can more fully experience the intimate fellowship with the heavenly Father that Jesus knew.

We want to draw your attention first to the significant phrase that introduces this passage: "in the days of His flesh." This expression emphasizes the human nature Christ embraced during His earthly ministry. That word *flesh* identifies Jesus with you and me; we have a Savior who can identify with us because of the human form that He assumed as He emptied Himself of His divine privileges and came to earth as a man (Philippians 2:7–8). As we study His prayer life, we're seeing Jesus *in His humanity* praying to the Father, just as we pray to Him in our own humanity.

A few verses earlier in Hebrews we read how Jesus, as our High Priest, can "sympathize with our weaknesses" because He "was in all points tempted as we are, yet without sin" (Hebrews 4:15). Whatever weaknesses, failings, and weariness we've ever experienced in our prayer life, *Christ understands!* He was tempted in His prayer life as well, and He knows how to help us faithfully resist those temptations in the same way He successfully resisted them.

SETTING OUR HEARTS

Our passage in Hebrews goes on to tell us that "in the days of His flesh," Jesus "offered up prayers and supplications, with vehement cries and tears...." (Hebrews 5:7). *The Amplified Bible* words it this way: "In the days of His flesh [Jesus] offered up definite, special petitions [for that which He not only wanted but needed] and supplications with strong crying and tears."

The clear emphasis is that the Son of God actively and

consistently *prayed!* And He did so with various kinds of prayer and supplication (strong entreaty and pleading) to His Father.

Being in agony,

He prayed more earnestly.

LUKE 22:44

In the days of His flesh, Jesus understood the seriousness of communicating with His heavenly Father. In the days of His flesh, He chose not to allow anything to discontinue or hamper that fellowship.

What can be said of your life—in the days of *your* flesh? Have you come to understand the importance of maintaining communication with God above everything else? What things have you let distract you from daily communication with the Father?

If Jesus was convinced that His own life and ministry depended upon His prayer life with the Father, we as well must set our hearts to maintain uninterrupted time in prayer with our Lord, for this is the key not only to our ministry but to our very life as God intends it.

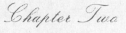

Chapter Two

THE HEART OF OUR PRAYER

We've seen how Christ's prayers were expressed "with vehement cries and tears" (Hebrews 5:7). Why was there such strong emotion in His praying?

It was because Jesus knew the Father's *love*—and sought to prevail upon that love in asking the Father to come to His aid. As our Savior acknowledged in prayer, *"You loved Me* before the foundation of the world" (John 17:24).

Jesus loved the Father and was loved by the Father! Therefore He confidently expected the Father to hear and answer His requests from a loving heart. And He knew that any and every answer from the Father would always be an expression of that love. Our Savior understood that everything the Father did in His life was out of a deep expression of love.

In the days of His flesh, Jesus fully grasped the importance of this love relationship. The Scriptures reveal that He and His Father were always in loving union and constant fellowship with each other. As Jesus often reminded His disciples, "I am in the Father, and the Father in Me" (John 14:10–11; see also 10:30,38; 14:20).

Jesus was intensely committed to prayer because this loving presence of the Father was *His very life*. He told His disciples, "I *live* because of the Father" (John 6:57)—and prayer was His lifeline. This vital closeness of the Son with the Father is the foremost characteristic of our Savior's prayer life.

It was a closeness that found expression in His constant time alone with the Father in prayer. Jesus allowed nothing to interfere or distract Him from this intimate fellowship—neither His family, nor His disciples, nor His religious critics and opponents. There was too much at stake.

The people around the Lord frequently didn't understand this close relationship between the Father and the Son, just as they failed often to grasp what kind of relationship they should have (for example, see Matthew 15:17; 16:9; Mark 8:17; 16:14; Luke 24:25). This is one reason that Jesus so often had to find solitary places and pray alone with the Father. But Jesus let nothing deter Him from maintaining His love relationship with the Father.

THROUGH THE HOLY SPIRIT

Jesus' intimacy with the Father in His prayer life was distinctively linked to the Holy Spirit, because He knew the Spirit's activity was the key to God's anointing and equipping for service in His kingdom.

The first time we see this profound link between Jesus, His prayers, the Holy Spirit, and the closeness of Father and Son is the moment of His baptism in the Jordan River: "It came to pass that Jesus also was baptized; and while He prayed, the heaven was opened. And the Holy Spirit descended in bodily form like a dove upon Him, and a voice came from heaven which said, 'You are My beloved Son; in You I am well pleased'" (Luke 3:21–22).

"How much more will your heavenly Father give the Holy Spirit to those who ask Him!"

LUKE 11:13

As Jesus prayed, the Holy Spirit came upon Him with enabling for the ministry that lay ahead, while the Father confirmed His love for His Son.

WHAT ABOUT YOU?

We can study closely this loving closeness between the heavenly Father and the Son, and even strongly admire this relationship—and yet fail to make the connection to our own lives.

What about you? Are you experiencing intimate fellowship with the heavenly Father in the days of your flesh? Throughout each day, as you carry out your responsibilities and activities, are you living in continual fellowship with the Son and with the Father, through the Holy Spirit? Can you say, "I am in Him, and He is in me"?

Have you, in prayer, allowed the Spirit to teach and shape you to the image of Christ so that you can say, "If you've seen me, you've seen my heavenly Father" as Jesus did (John 14:9)? Have you spent enough time in prayer to know that your words and works are the words and works of the Father, as Jesus did (John 14:10)?

He departed to the mountain to pray.

MARK 6:46

As you pursue a closer relationship with God through prayer, are you keeping the Father's love in the forefront of your thinking and experience? When we pray, we must remember that God loves us, has plans for us, and will lay His heart over our hearts as we pray.

Just as Jesus did, we must find regular times of solitary prayer to receive the Father's direction for our lives. We can not allow distractions to interfere. (If you've walked with the Lord for even a short time, you know how easy it can be to get distracted from this priority!) Nor can we become discouraged if others don't understand our closeness with the heavenly Father and all that He is telling us.

CONFIDENCE AND JOY

Jesus understood that every Christian needs to maintain this fellowship to be able to serve and honor our Lord in this world. He was so deeply convinced of this that He made the following request on behalf of His followers: "that they all may be one, as You, Father, are in Me, and I in You; *that they also may be one in Us*" (John 17:21).

Many other passages illustrate this unity and fellowship we're to experience with our Lord. In John 15:5, Jesus said, "I am the vine, you are the branches," and He spoke of this close relationship as our "abiding" in Him. He immediately tied this to prayer: "If you abide in Me, and

My words abide in you, you will ask what you desire, and it shall be done for you" (v. 7).

Jesus knew that when we experience this loving relationship with the Lord, it brings confidence into our prayer lives—a confidence that leads to joy: "These things I have spoken to you, that My joy may remain in you, and that your joy may be full" (John 15:11).

PRAYER STARTS WITH RELATIONSHIP

When the disciples in Luke 11 asked Jesus, "Lord, teach us to pray" (v. 1), He gave them a brief model or pattern for prayer—what we know as "the Lord's Prayer." It's not some kind of magic formula, but a concise portrayal of the foundational truths that should be in our minds and hearts as we pray individually, as families, and as churches.

Every phrase in this prayer pattern is significant, especially the opening words. Jesus taught His disciples to say, *"Our Father in heaven…"* (Luke 11:2).

Jesus Himself repeatedly addressed God as "Father" (Matthew 11:25; Mark 14:36; Luke 23:46; John 17:1)— and here He encourages the disciples to do the same. He was teaching them that intimacy with God is what we should all experience when we pray. Prayer is not repeating routine words (Matthew 6:7) or trying to impress those around us with our spirituality (Matthew 6:5); prayer is meant to flow from close and vital fellowship with the heavenly Father.

At the same time, the words "in heaven" teach us that God is holy and that we must approach Him with respect. He is in heaven while we still remain upon the earth.

There's a wonderful balance in what Jesus teaches here. We intimately call upon God as Father, while those words "in heaven" remind us also of His infinite greatness and the vast realm of His presence and activity. "In heaven" brings to mind as well the immensity of everything He possesses as Sovereign over all things. As we come to God in prayer, we come to our loving Father who remains on His throne with all the resources of heaven and earth at His disposal on our behalf.

Jesus knew that heaven and earth are closely tied together. God is present *here;* His rule on earth is real, personal, and sovereign, and His help can be counted on. And He wants *us* to know this as well.

And while He prayed...

heaven was opened.

LUKE 3:21

How deep is your relationship with the Lord as you pray? Do you pour your heart out to Him with complete confidence and trust in His help, because you've come to know and experience His love?

This isn't something we can start practicing automatically—it takes effort and time, like any relationship. The more you spend time with Him, the more you'll come to understand His ways, His heart, and His will as you pray. There's no substitute for taking time to study the Bible and for allowing the Holy Spirit to teach you how to pray in a way consistent with God's will. Place His Word in your heart and mind…then the Holy Spirit will use those Scriptures as you pray to keep your life on track and consistent with God's nature.

Chapter Three

OUR PURPOSE IN PRAYER

*P*rayer is not for the purpose of getting God to help us…but for getting us in line with what God is about to do. Prayer is God's invitation to enter His throne room so He can lay *His agenda* over our hearts.

To clearly see this truth in practice, there's nothing better than observing the prayer life of Jesus.

A HEART OF REVERENT SUBMISSION

At the center of our Savior's prayer life was His seeking after the Father's purposes, activities, and heart. Jesus sought His Father's heart not just for information, but for personal instruction.

In Hebrews 5 we read that when Jesus prayed to His Father in the days of His flesh, He "was heard because of His godly fear" (v. 7). *The Amplified Bible* expresses this as "because of His reverence toward God [His godly fear, His piety]." Other translations render it, "because of his reverent submission" (NIV), and "because of his reverence" (ESV).

This passage makes it clear that Jesus was heard because of the submissive attitude of His heart towards the Father—He had already fully yielded His life to the Father's will. God always reads the heart when we pray and always knows our relationship with Him as we pray. And He responds to us according to that relationship.

The heart of the Son was to learn His assignment from the Father and to reverently surrender to it. He had set His heart to obey even before He prayed. Jesus entered prayer with godly fear and reverent submission toward God's will—with a sense of *divine accountability*—and this submissive heart merited the "ear" of the Father to the Son.

What's your attitude of heart as you come to God in prayer? Do you find yourself arguing with the Lord when

He knelt down and prayed.

LUKE 22:41

He brings an assignment? Does "self" raise its head to rebel when you even hear that word *submit?* If so, don't expect God to hear or answer your prayers. God doesn't give a large or challenging assignment to someone with an unsubmissive heart. He knows us and has already determined His answer before we pray.

Have you resolved that no matter what God reveals to you and requests of you through prayer, your answer is an unqualified *yes,* even before He shows you? This is the heart of what we see in Jesus' reverent submission. The Father knew this and was always ready to hear and answer the prayers of the Son.

For Jesus, prayer wasn't simply talking with God, but involved a deep, abiding sense of reverent submission to Him. Therefore, every time Jesus entered His Father's presence, the Father opened His Son's understanding to what He, the Father, was doing—so that Jesus could immediately adjust His life to it, and the Father could continue to accomplish His purposes for the world through Him.

Through His prayer life, Jesus always knew the Father's intentions. The prayers of Jesus released His life to the Father's will.

Let's observe some of the evidence in Scripture of how Jesus sought this direction from the Father through prayer.

In the opening chapter of Mark's Gospel we read this about Jesus: "Now in the morning, having risen a long while before daylight, He went out and departed to a solitary place; and there He prayed" (Mark 1:35).

In its context, this is a very remarkable thing that Jesus did. In the earlier verses of this chapter, we read that He had just put in an extremely full day and evening of ministry in the city of Capernaum—teaching, preaching, healing, and casting out demons. It would be an exhausting schedule for anyone. And yet after what must have been only a few hours' sleep at most, the Savior got up long before daybreak to pray to the Father.

We aren't told what Jesus prayed in those early hours, but what happens next is very instructive.

Simon Peter and others came looking for Jesus. After finding Him, they told Him, "Everyone is looking for You" (Mark 1:37). That would have been no surprise to Jesus; He had spent the previous day teaching people and healing those who were sick, and they understandably wanted to see and experience more of His power and authority and compassion. But Jesus' response at this point was surprising: "Let us go into the next towns, that I may preach there also, because for this purpose I have come forth" (1:38).

How did Jesus know He was not to stay in Capernaum

but to go elsewhere? Because He had heard from His Father! He had been up before dawn, praying. And in those dark and still hours, the Father had instructed the Son that He was not sent to meet whatever needs people perceived and expressed. Rather, He had been sent to do the will of the Father, and the Father had clearly set before Him a bigger task than just the external needs of people in Capernaum.

This isn't to say that such needs aren't important. Certainly, the neediness of those around us will always press in on anyone being used of God. Jesus was moved to compassion by the needs He saw (Matthew 14:14), and He ministered to the crowds everywhere He went. The example of our Lord showed continually that people's needs were met as He obeyed the Father. But He didn't let these needs sidetrack Him from His larger assignment.

In the same manner, our time alone with God in prayer will keep us from turning aside from the Savior's will for our lives, and will give us confidence to remain faithful to God's assignment when other people interrupt and try to get us on their own agenda.

He was alone praying.

LUKE 9:18

From Henry: Settling the "Pulls" on Our Lives

Throughout my ministry, there have been many times when others have said they "knew" I needed to either join something they were involved in or follow what they were "suggesting." Many times, their suggestions involved worthy activities or causes that were quite significant and helpful. Many times they represented an opportunity that, on the surface, was something I *wanted* to be involved in.

At such times, prayer is always the place where I settle these pulls on my life.

The choices I face are rarely between a good option and a bad one, but rather between two exciting opportunities. However, I have one Lord. He alone must direct me, and unless I've heard specifically from Him that I should change direction from what He has earlier called me to, I must say no to other people's suggestions for my life.

Sometimes when I say no to these requests, people get offended and feel that I've rejected them. But it isn't a matter of rejecting them or their suggestions; it's a matter of hearing from my Lord and remaining obedient to Him.

When someone approaches me to express God's will for my life, my response is always, "If God told you, then we can trust Him to tell me as well."

We must seek this direction for our lives in the same way Jesus did, looking to the Father alone for each assignment.

Part of the Father's will for the Savior was to give Him twelve men as apostles to whom Jesus could teach the things of God. To His Father, Jesus spoke of these twelve as "the men whom You have given Me" in His great high priestly prayer recorded in John 17. "They were Yours," He said, and "You gave them to Me" (v. 6).

How did Jesus know that these particular men had been given to Him by the Father?

Luke's Gospel tells us that on the night before He selected these twelve as apostles, Jesus spent "all night in prayer to God" (Luke 6:12). That's how important this decision was to Him. And during this night of prayer, the Father showed His Son exactly which twelve men to select.

Jesus was summoned to prayer so that the Father could let Him know what He was about to do—to give Him the men who were to be the "foundation" upon which God would build His church (Ephesians 2:20) and reach out and touch the world with His salvation.

Only the understanding from the Father in prayer could prepare the Son for receiving the gift of these men and for knowing how He was to relate with each one.

In the same manner that the Father instructed the Son, He also desires to instruct us. Have you been willing to spend time in prayer at the front end of every assignment in order to gain God's perspective and instruction?

When was the last time you spent all night in prayer in order to receive the wisdom of God for your life?

A MOMENT OF ULTIMATE SUBMISSION

The climax of Christ's "reverent submission" to the Father in prayer came in Gethsemane, with these words: "Nevertheless, not as I will, but as You will" (Matthew 26:39). Here is the ultimate, transparent moment of reverent submission in godly fear in Jesus' life of prayer.

This is also the moment that comes first to mind when we read the summary of Jesus' prayer life in Hebrews 5:7–9—when we see Jesus offering "vehement cries and tears to Him who was able to save Him from death." As Jesus entered Gethsemane, He told His disciples, "My soul is exceedingly sorrowful, even to death" (Mark 14:34). In Luke we read that this sorrow and agony was so great that "His sweat became like great drops of blood falling down to the ground" (Luke 22:44). In such anguish over what He was about to face, His pain was real as He repeatedly prayed, "O My Father, if it is possible, let this cup pass from Me"—but He always added, "Not as I will, but as You will" (Matthew 26:39).

Jesus prayed this way in Gethsemane because of the load the Father was asking Him to carry—the sin of the

From Henry: **Praying All Night**

I have often, over the years, spent all night in prayer for each of my five children and now fourteen grandchildren.

I've also told my children, "Always give God your best; He is God and is worthy of your best." I haven't tried to tell them what their best is or what it will look like—only that if they would seek God with all their heart, He would show them what that is and how they're to follow Him.

I've always encouraged them to know that as they give God their best, He'll be faithful to guide and enable them to serve Him.

It has been a joy to watch each of our children give God their best in their preparation for ministry, as all four of my sons have earned doctorates, and our daughter has received her master's degree from seminary. Now Marilynn and I are watching them give God their best in ministry.

world! Jesus understood what this would involve and require from Him, and He knew that only through the strength and guidance from the heavenly Father would He be able to fulfill the Father's will. Only through ongoing, intimate fellowship with "Him who was able to save Him from death" could He commit Himself to carrying this load that was asked of Him.

And how did Jesus know that this was the load He should carry?

Because in prayer with the Father, the Son had been informed of the task at hand, its timing, and its means, as well as the strength needed to complete His mission. Therefore He was in deep anguish over the events He would have to immediately face, but He knew the end result would be the defeat of sin and death for mankind.

Do you know what load God has for you to carry today? If you're a child of God, then you're a servant of God; have you spent enough time with your Master to be instructed for His plans and purposes set aside for your life?

Again He went away and prayed,

and spoke the same words.

MARK 14:39

In the midst of a hurting and troubled world, have you maintained a singleness of mind to hear your mission from God, just as Jesus did?

FOR GOD'S KINGDOM AND GOD'S WILL

Jesus taught us to seek God's will in this way in the prayer that He gave His disciples. He told us to pray, "Your kingdom come" (Luke 11:2).

Jesus' greatest desire was for God's sovereign rule to be done in all things in and through His life. We must also have this same desire, and express it in our prayers. God must have the same unhindered access to our lives for His kingdom purposes.

Jesus also told us to pray, "Your will be done on earth as it is in heaven" (Luke 11:2). God's kingdom comes on earth when God's will is done on earth. We know God's will is done in heaven, because there's nothing in heaven to hinder it. Jesus is saying, "Pray that the same perfect accomplishment of the Father's will in heaven may also be accomplished on earth." Heaven comes very close to those who have submitted their hearts to the will of God in prayer.

The phrases in the Lord's Prayer remind us that our minds and hearts are deeply affected by sin, and sin strongly affects our ability to pray, so that "we do not know what we should pray for as we ought" (Romans 8:26). By example and teaching, Jesus helps us by showing us what to pray for. If we are careful to release our wills to Him in prayer and to set our hearts to give God unhindered access to our lives, we'll keep our prayers from being self-centered and outside the will of God.

We are *His* servants; He is not our servant to do for us as we desire. Though in all things we can have confidence that He hears and responds to our requests (1 John 5:14–15), we must always ask according to His will.

RECEIVING GOD'S AGENDA

When you're praying either alone or with others and God is speaking to you, don't bring up your own agenda. Instead, shift your heart to receive *His* agenda.

The importance of this is illustrated by the response of Jesus' disciples at a critical moment in His earthly ministry.

WHEN WE FAIL TO LISTEN

Jesus took Peter, James, and John and "led them up on a high mountain by themselves; and He was transfigured before them" (Matthew 17:1–2). While the physical presence of Jesus was blazing with supernatural light, two men, Moses and Elijah, "appeared in glory" to talk with the Savior. They "spoke of His decease which He was about to accomplish at Jerusalem" (Luke 9:29–31). In this incredible moment, they addressed what God was about to do in the death and resurrection of Jesus. The whole focus of this time was on the Father's purpose to set the world free from sin.

But the disciples missed God's agenda at this key time. Scripture records Peter's reaction: "Then Peter answered and said to Jesus, 'Lord, it is good for us to be here; if You wish, let us make here three tabernacles: one for You, one for Moses, and one for Elijah'" (Matthew 17:4). While God was discussing the release of the whole world from the bondage of our sin, all Peter could think about was erecting a building.

No wonder the Father responded as He did. While Peter "was still speaking, behold, a bright cloud overshadowed them; and suddenly a voice came out of the cloud, saying, 'This is My beloved Son, in whom I am well pleased. Hear Him!'" (Matthew 17:5). God was saying in effect, "When the Lord starts to speak, *you keep quiet! Don't tell Him what you think is best. Listen to Him!*"

Peter's lack of humble listening was nothing new for God's people. All through the Bible, they tried to tell Him what to do.

At that time Jesus answered and said,
"I thank You, Father,
Lord of heaven and earth...."
MATTHEW 11:25

EXPERIENCING PRAYER WITH JESUS

The same is true for us. Many times we're not good listeners when we pray. We'd rather tell God our latest ideas and plans. But if we listen, we may hear the Lord telling us what He told Job, when He said in essence, "Where were you when I created the worlds? Did you counsel Me back then? Did you tell Me how to establish the world and set the stars in place? Did you counsel Me when I put together the seas and the mountains?" (Job 38).

Hearing this, Job responded in humility before God (Job 40:3–5; 42:1–6), and our response should be similar when we're tempted to tell God how to run His ministry: "O Lord, forgive my ignorance. Who am I to tell You what I think is best in redeeming a world? I didn't lay down my life. You did! It was *Your* Son and His blood that brought our redemption. And it was *Your* Holy Spirit that You poured out on Your people to give them resurrection life and power. Who am I to tell You how to bring this world to Yourself? You alone know, O Lord."

THE LORD'S MANY GOOD PURPOSES
FOR OUR LIVES

The Father continues to have specific purposes for each of our lives which He desires to accomplish as part of His eternal purposes for all of creation. Several key Scriptures highlight this vital truth.

In the Old Testament, God expresses His heart to us through the prophet Jeremiah: "For I know the thoughts that I think toward you, says the LORD, thoughts of peace and not of evil, to give you a future and a hope" (Jeremiah 29:11). These "thoughts" God has for us represent His agenda for us, His plans and purposes on our behalf, and we must understand that all these are for our good. We can know that no matter what we ask in prayer, God's perfect love will not (and cannot) give us second best. He will not give us anything contrary to His determined will, though He is sovereign and able to grant anything. He is committed to His loving plans and purposes for us.

Our discovery of these plans and purposes is inseparably linked with intimate prayer to God, just as this passage in Jeremiah quickly points out: "Then you will call upon Me and go and pray to Me, and I will listen to you. And you will seek Me and find Me, when you search for Me with all your heart. I will be found by you, says the LORD" (Jeremiah 29:12–14).

We get a glimpse of the vastness of these thoughts God has toward us by reading David's words in the Psalms: "How precious also are Your thoughts to me, O God! How great is the sum of them! If I should count them, they would be more in number than the sand" (Psalm 139:17–18).

Many times when we pray, our focus isn't on understanding the Father's purposes, activities, and heart. Instead, we pray for our needs to be met without considering His eternal plans, or we let God know how we want Him to make us successful.

When you pray, are you on your own agenda, or listening to His? When was the last time you came to God in prayer, and even before you opened your mouth there was already an absolute, unconditional submission? Let this be your heart's desire: "Lord, whatever You say, my answer is yes, because that's the only worthy response to You."

What is God talking to you about when you pray? Not what are you talking to Him about, but what is He speaking with you about? What is the last thing God said to you when you went before Him in prayer? Are you communicating with the Lord to know without any question what He has purposed for you? Do you know the eternal significance of it all?

Are you finding that He's opening your understanding as He comes alongside you to let you know what is on His agenda? Are you staying long enough in the Father's presence to allow Him to reveal to you His ways, truths, understanding, and agenda? Have you waited long enough before Him to know what it will cost you to carry out the assignment?

Seeking and submitting to God's agenda doesn't mean that we don't openly take our needs and requests to our Father in heaven. We must never hesitate to pray even the most extensive requests. But we must learn to release our own agendas and with an honest heart say, "Not my will, but Yours be done." We need to always approach God with a heart that wants nothing more than His will to be accomplished. And we must have the confidence that His purposes are so much larger than our requests or our perspective regarding any present need.

The Lord isn't interested in us disciplining ourselves to "say our prayers"; the Pharisees had their prayers down cold, but they were absolutely useless to God. What God is looking for is a heart that's increasingly responsive to His touch. Not for you to tell God how devoted you are by all of your religious activities, but for you to recognize that when you enter into God's throne room, one touch from Him brings an immediate response from you, and the immediate results of your prayer will be obedience to His will.

When we learn what the Lord's specific will is and receive His guidance for our next assignment, this does not mean that the next steps will be easy. Often there is difficulty quickly awaiting us. We often hear testimonies to the reality of this in people's lives as they seek the Father; many times there is great intensity of heart once God reveals His will.

Don't be thrown off by the intensity of the struggle and agony you may experience in your own prayer life. Remember again how our Lord and Savior, on that dark night in Gethsemane, was determined to obey and honor the Father, while at the same time He felt the terrible weight of the assignment and brought His heavy heart to the Father.

So don't be discouraged if your heart becomes sorrowful as you cry out to God in the assignment He has placed you. Your Savior understands and relates to you during this time. In a relationship with our heavenly Father who loves us and is in complete control of all things, there are times when we simply need to present our heart and thoughts to Him. Who better can we share the burdens of our heart with than our heavenly Father?

He left them, went away again, and prayed.

MATTHEW 26:44

When the pain comes, follow the example of Christ and cry out to the only One who can bring understanding, strength, and comfort to your life. Take heart that in the midst of the pain, the love of the Father in heaven surrounds you and will prepare and empower you to keep going. There will be many times when you find yourself crying out to the Lord with deep concerns of your heart as you follow Him, but you can be confident in the Father's love to hear and answer your prayers as you submit your life to Him.

If, however, you've been a Christian for a long period of time and have never experienced anguish of soul as God has sought to use your life, then ask the Lord if you've truly been submitting your life to the Father for His service. There's a cost to denying self, taking up a cross, and following after our Lord (Luke 9:23). If God did not spare His Son from agony of soul, then we shouldn't expect Him to spare us from the cost of being His disciple.

THE FEAR OF THE LORD

Anyone who spends significant time in prayer with God, as Jesus did, will come to know the heart of God. Knowing the heart of God is to know the will of God, and to know the will of God is to tremble before Him with an awesome sense of accountability—as reflected in the godly fear, the reverent submission with which Jesus came to His Father in prayer in the days of His flesh (Hebrews 5:7–8).

This fear, this sense of accountability, is one of the great missing elements in the prayers of many people today, and typically it's a result of the loss of intimacy with God in prayer.

This awesome sense of accountability is "the fear of the Lord" mentioned so often in the Scriptures, the same fear of the Lord which is "the beginning of wisdom" (Psalm 111:10; Proverbs 9:10). To fear the Lord is to "hate evil" and to "depart from evil" (Proverbs 8:13; 3:7). "In the fear of the LORD there is strong confidence," for "the fear of the LORD is a fountain of life" (Proverbs 14:26–27), and for those who fear Him, "there is no want" (Psalm 34:9).

David reminds us that for the wicked person, "there is no fear of God before his eyes. For he flatters himself in his own eyes" (Psalm 36:1–2). Tragically, this same attitude is common among Christians in their prayer lives. If you use your prayer time to instruct God on what you think you need and want, instead of coming before the Lord in prayer with an awesome sense of accountability to obey all that He instructs during your prayer time, then there's no fear of the One to whom you're praying.

In our day the meaning of the word *fear* has become

restricted to negative emotions and actions. The idea of having fear toward a loving God is unacceptable to many people. But Christ taught that a healthy fear of God would help His followers to remain faithful to the calling the Father had placed on their lives. When Jesus was sending out the disciples to proclaim the Good News and warned them of the coming persecution from the world, He told them not to fear men who could harm them physically, but to fear God who held their eternal destiny in His hand (Matthew 10:28). This fear would help them remain faithful to the gospel in the face of difficulties.

But in the same breath with which the Master charged His disciples to fear God, He also reminded them that their Father in heaven cared for them and loved them, so that they were not to have a negative fear: "Are not two sparrows sold for a copper coin? And not one of them falls to the ground apart from your Father's will. But the very hairs of your head are all numbered. *Do not fear therefore;* you are of more value than many sparrows" (Matthew 10:29–31).

He went a little farther
and fell on His face, and prayed.
MATTHEW 26:39

EXPERIENCING PRAYER WITH JESUS

Jesus had no difficulty connecting a proper fear of God with knowing God's love. For us, such a comprehensive understanding can come only through intimate fellowship with the Father through prayer and Bible study. As each of us seeks the heart of God through the Scriptures, prayer provides an intimate fellowship with the Author of Scripture to reinforce His love towards us as expressed in the Bible. This deep awareness of accountability to God for eternal things will then characterize your prayer life.

As you spend time in prayer, your knowledge of God will continue to grow. Not only will you come to understand the will of God expressed in your life, but you'll come to understand the character of God—His holiness, His love, His heart, His ways, and His words. As you're exposed to the things of God in prayer, it will also create within you a holy fear of God.

WHY REVIVAL TARRIES

We are convinced that revival in our land waits upon God's people coming to Him, personally and collectively, in prayer that is marked by this kind of reverent submission and fear of God.

Our society and culture is at a point where we believe that Christians need to let the prayer life of Jesus penetrate us until we're on God's agenda when we pray. Then what happened when Jesus prayed will happen for us: Heaven and earth will be joined together, and the words we hear from the Father will center around how God is going to carry out the deliverance of the whole world through the proclamation of the gospel.

Could it be that God's invitation to you and me in the days to come is to let us in on such a conversation from heaven? Could it be that He's about to bring release from the bondage of sin in our nation and world and to bring a great spiritual revival?

The historical events in recent years have included so many tragedies of epic proportion, bringing many reminders of the powerful hold of darkness upon our world. Every time one of these major events happens, it gives us a spiritual wake-up call. We sense God asking us all, "Do you know what could be prevented if you would only pray?"

In such a time as this—in these days of our flesh—what could be more important for us than to understand what is on the heart of God regarding revival and spiritual awakening in our land and in our world?

Chapter Five

OUR APPROACH IN PRAYER

We've been studying key characteristics of Jesus' prayer life, in particular His utmost determination to seek the Father's heart and will.

There are also other characteristics of Jesus' prayer life that compel our closer look, so we can understand and apply them to our lives. We feel these characteristics are crucial for Christians to understand and practice in our day.

A HABIT OF TIME

We've already noted how Jesus was in the habit of going in prayer to His Father in the early morning hours. We never sense that our Lord found these regular times in prayer becoming stale and needing a "change-up" to keep them fresh. Instead, we get the sense that these prayer times were His lifeline.

There's nothing routine about meeting and talking

with our Lord. To know that each day you'll be meeting with the Creator of the universe who has words of life as well as daily guidance for you is a source of joy, strength, and hope.

A regular time of prayer, especially in the morning hours, prepares your heart and makes you sensitive to the ways and things of God. It prepares you for what you'll face in the day. God knows what your day holds and He'll instruct you before you face difficult situations. The God who created the universe, who created you, and who orchestrates your day is more than capable of preparing you for anything if you'll spend the necessary time with Him.

We have learned that the Scriptures He brings to mind during our time of prayer and Bible study in the mornings, and the people and concerns that the Lord impresses on our heart in this time, will directly apply to the events of the coming day. Throughout the day, each event, each conversation, and each person encountered will in some way be connected with what the Lord spoke to us while we were in prayer.

A HABIT OF PLACE

A regular place for times of prayer is also important. We read that when Jesus was in Jerusalem, the garden of

Gethsemane on the Mount of Olives was His "accustomed" place of prayer (Luke 22:39); John tells us that "Jesus often met there with His disciples" (John 18:2), presumably to pray with them as well as to privately teach them. In fact, it was because Jesus was frequently in this location that Judas knew where to lead the soldiers in order to arrest Him on the night he betrayed the Savior (John 18:2).

He was praying in a certain place.

LUKE 11:1

Having a regular place and time for prayer was true also of the prophet Daniel. When King Darius signed the decree to outlaw the worship of anyone other than himself, Daniel's enemies knew when and where to wait in order to catch Daniel in prayer, "as was his custom since early days" (Daniel 6:10–11).

Over the years, we have found that setting aside a regular time of prayer in a set location has become an exciting time of daily refreshing. What about you? Do you have a regular time and place for personal prayer?

What does your routine reveal about the importance of prayer in your life? Do people close to you know of your routines for prayer? Have you established prayer in your life to such a degree that your spouse, your children, and your closest friends will know where and when to find you in prayer?

We often hear people argue that setting aside a specific time and place for prayer can become legalistic. Some feel that this can make a person's prayer life routine and limited. But having a specific time and place to pray doesn't mean you don't have an active, spontaneous prayer life throughout the day. In fact, your heart to pray during the day is only enhanced by a routine of uninterrupted prayer and a set location.

PRAYER WITH INTENSITY

We've seen how Jesus, in the days of His flesh, prayed to His Father "with vehement cries and tears" (Hebrews 5:7). Reading this verse, one stands in awe and wonder. Imagine the Son of God praying this way to the Father! This was intense, excruciating prayer, and we see it especially in Gethsemane.

On that night in the garden, Jesus was assured of the Father's love for Him; He knew the Father would strengthen Him for the assignment that was facing Him; and He was fully confident that He was completely in the

From Norman: A Prayer Routine for Parents

I've found that I must get into my office before others arrive in the morning in order to have an unhurried time in prayer and Bible study.

And in our home, our children know that the daily routine begins with their mother getting up very early to pray and read her Bible. Our children are seeing that prayer is important because by the time they get out of bed, they know their mom has already spent a long time in prayer before she begins her day.

Father's will. But all this didn't diminish the intensity of the prayers He offered. This intensity came from One who had absolute confidence in the heavenly Father.

How would you describe the intensity of your own prayer life? Can you say that your petitions and supplication to the Father are marked by "cries and tears"?

When you think of Jesus in prayer in Gethsemane—only hours away from dying for the sins of the world—do you think that there's any less intensity in God's heart today for those who are lost and facing an eternity apart from God? Is sin and its destruction any less offensive or real in our day than it was in Jesus' day?

The servants of God should experience a deep intensity in their seeking after God in prayer. As our world heads morally downward, are there vehement cries and tears in our churches for God's strength to carry out their assignment to be salt and light among the nations? Or have we lost this intensity?

What do we have on our hearts when we come to pray as individuals and as churches? In Gethsemane, Jesus was totally focused on what lay before Him, with no hint of any distraction of any kind. What about us? Have we become sidetracked or casual about our assignment as Christians, and in turn lost the passion of Christlike praying? Could this be why there are so few "vehement cries and tears" when we pray alone or when our churches are praying?

FINDING SUPPORT FROM OTHERS

We've seen how Jesus had a habit of strategically going alone into a solitary place to pray and to receive daily instruction. But in Gethsemane we see also how Jesus brought along His closest companions to pray with Him. When God's people pray through the sorrowful times, it's crucial that we bring others along to help carry the load of following our Lord.

Of the twelve men whom the Father had given Jesus as apostles, three were entrusted with "going deeper" with Him, especially in sharing His prayer life. At Gethsemane,

Now it came to pass...
that He took Peter, John, and James
and went up on the mountain to pray.
LUKE 9:28

He took these three—Peter, James, and John—further into the garden to pray, and He shared with them His anguish of heart: "My soul is exceedingly sorrowful, even to death" (Matthew 26:38). This was not incidental, but crucial.

Peter, James, and John had the privilege of coming close to Jesus as He prayed about the awesome burden He was carrying, and thus helping Jesus through this critical moment. This was their assignment. No doubt the Savior intended them to learn things from this experience that they would need to have in place as they later led the early church. But in this crucial hour, instead of watching and praying with Him they fell asleep and had to be reminded by the Savior of the weakness of their flesh (Matthew 26:41).

Although they failed in their assignment at this moment, the example of Jesus in seeking their support still holds. In times of deep distress, the Lord brought others close to Him to help carry His burden.

This is a vital aspect of praying for us as well. And yet when Christians today face the deep burdens and the pain that often come with following God's will, many times they choose to do it alone.

Do you have those companions around you who can help you carry the burdens of your heart to the Lord?

For exploring further another characteristic of Jesus' prayer life, let's return to the opening words of the model prayer He gave His disciples. Jesus taught them to pray, "Hallowed be Your name" (Luke 11:2).

In Jesus' day a person's name carried much greater significance than in our day. The name was thought to be bound up with the person as a reflection of the very nature of their personality. The name and the activity of a person were tied together. "Hallowed be Your name" was therefore a prayer to keep God's name holy and to hold it in proper reverence in our hearts and minds, and through daily living that reflects His holy name and character.

It's important to understand that this request was the very first request in this pattern of prayer that Jesus taught. How we approach God and treat His name will set the tone for our praying.

Often we come to God and express our heart without considering His name and nature. Think carefully about what you're asking of the Father in prayer. Is it consistent with what Scripture has revealed about His ways and His nature?

Keeping this in mind will often change the entire focus of your praying. Knowing, at the front end of your praying, that your heart's desire is for your life to present His name and character as holy to a watching world will cause you to speak and listen more carefully in prayer.

Jesus hallowed the Father's name by always praying in a way consistent with God's nature, ways, purposes, and especially His Will. He would never pray anything contrary to the nature of God. This is where we must *think* both before we pray and while we pray. This will help keep us from praying outside the Father's revealed will and nature, or outside Jesus' commands and truth, or outside what we know of the Holy Spirit's nature and activity.

A HOLY HUSH

In the Scriptures, those who knew they were in the presence of God often fell face down with no strength left in them. But today, so many have lost the awe of coming before God in prayer. They forget that He is not a common buddy, but a holy God. We ought to have a holy hush before Him.

When was the last time you quietly entered the presence of God and there came over you such a sense of awe that you could hardly open your mouth?

Let Christ's teaching as well as His example continue to teach to properly revere the holy name of God.

Chapter Six

PRAYING FOR OTHERS

*S*o far in this book we've concentrated mostly on the personal aspect in prayer of discovering and receiving the Lord's agenda for our individual lives.

But of course Scripture clearly commands us to pray also for others. "I exhort first of all," Paul wrote to Timothy, "that supplications, prayers, intercessions, and giving of thanks be made *for all men*" (1 Timothy 2:1). We're told to be "praying always with all prayer and supplication in the Spirit, being watchful to this end with all perseverance and supplication *for all the saints*" (Ephesians 6:18).

This kind of faithful, Spirit-led, persevering praying for others is an unmistakable mark of the prayer life of Jesus. His prayer life was supremely characterized by intercession for others.

We see this characteristic especially in the Savior's faithful prayer for His disciples. As Jesus came to know the Father's will, he exhibited a strong accountability to always be alert and watchful over the ones who had been entrusted to Him. He knew their weaknesses and knew they would face trials and temptations, and out of this awareness He prayed to the Father on their behalf. Because the Father revealed "all things" (John 5:20) to the Son, Jesus knew the need to be in prayer for the disciples.

We see, for example, the time when Jesus warned Simon Peter that severe testing would come, but also assured him of His prayers for him: "Simon, Simon! Indeed, Satan has asked for you, that he may sift you as wheat. But *I have prayed for you*, that your faith should not fail" (Luke 22:31–32).

Jesus' intercession for His followers is seen most clearly in His great high priestly prayer of John 17, where He prays not only for the Twelve but for all who would become followers of Christ down through the ages, including us. In this prayer, Jesus reviews with the Father His stewardship of the disciples' lives. First, He acknowledged that they belonged to the Father: "They were *Yours*" (John 17:6). As such, these disciples were infinitely precious to the Father, for they were His "special treasure" (Exodus

19:5). Jesus knew He was handling God's treasure, and this is reflected in His praying for them.

Second, Jesus knew that this treasure had been specifically entrusted to Him by the Father: "They were Yours, *You gave them to Me*" (John 17:6). It was in light of this awesome stewardship that Jesus interceded for His followers.

Third, Jesus had a clearly defined focus in His intercession: "I do not pray for the world but *for those whom You have given Me,* for they are Yours" (17:9). This was not prayer for the world, but prayer for those through whom the world would be reached.

"I pray for them."

JOHN 17:9

THE PLAN FOR THE WORLD'S REDEMPTION

When you look at the way in which Jesus spent His time while on earth, He was far more concerned for His disciples than for the "world." This doesn't mean of course that He wasn't concerned with the world, but He placed a huge emphasis on the people of God and specifically those who were His disciples. The reason for this emphasis was their importance in God's will for the world's redemption. This redemption would depend on the faithfulness of His followers to live out and proclaim the gospel. That was the Father's eternal plan and purpose: the salvation of the world, resting on the condition of His people.

Knowing this plan, Jesus interceded for His followers with great earnestness, especially in John 17. He said to the Father, "I do not pray that You should take them out of the world, but that You should keep them from the evil one" (17:15). And He prayed, "Sanctify them by Your truth" (17:17).

Jesus expressed to the Father His great awareness of the significance of these disciples to God and of His stewardship of their lives: "As You sent Me into the world, I also have sent them into the world" (17:18). So much is found in this statement! As Jesus held in His own life the great salvation God had planned for the entire world, so the lives of these disciples, entrusted to the Savior, would hold the key to taking the good news of God's salvation to all the nations. One without the other was—and continues to be—incomplete.

The disciples were to be sent into the very midst of the lost world, rather than being kept away or apart from this world's troubles. In this assignment they would face every form of struggle and challenge to their faith. If the disciples were to falter or turn away from God's will, eternity would be impacted.

Therefore Jesus, after affirming to the Father His stewardship of His disciples, asks for the Father's full affirmation of His life and ministry with His disciples, "that the world may know that You have sent Me, and have loved them as You have loved Me" (John 17:23).

OUR PATTERN FOR INTERCESSION

This intercession of Jesus for the disciples is a wonderful pattern for our intercession too. But this pattern in Jesus' prayer life is often tragically missing in our praying today, especially when the church is praying together. We pray earnestly for the "lost," but often neglect God's own children whom He has entrusted to us.

The believers are God's treasure, and they're precious to Him. Any neglect of them, especially in intercession, is an enormous failure on our part.

THE RIGHT TRAINING AT THE RIGHT TIME

In His prayer for His disciples, Jesus relied on the Father for an understanding of how to train and instruct them.

From Henry: **Interceding for Our Children**

Marilynn and I have watched this pattern of intercession for others in Jesus' life and applied it to our family. If Jesus was entrusted with the Twelve and was faithful to speak to them and teach them all that the Father had revealed for them to learn, then we also saw this as our goal as parents.

We prayed much for our children, believing that they are not ours, but given as a trust by the Father. God has a purpose for their lives and placed them in our home for instruction. To this end we prayed to the Father, and at times we spent all night in prayer for them, asking God, "What are the words you would have us speak to them?"

Our five children are now grown and have families of their own. But we continue to go to the Father in prayer and ask what He would have us speak to them.

As we've sought the Lord in prayer for instruction to share with our children, all five of them know God's purpose in their lives and are living for His eternal purposes and glory.

We still have a long way to go, and as we press on, prayer will always have a huge place in our lives on their behalf.

Jesus knew He had been given the assignment of instructing the apostles as He headed toward the cross.

There was no part of the Lord's ministry that wasn't directed by the Father through prayer. The Father not only gave instructions to Jesus as to what to teach them, but also revealed to Jesus when their training was over. In fact, Jesus did not move toward the cross until the Father had revealed to Him that the disciples had been convinced of the Savior's true identity. They would need to have this truth imbedded in their hearts by God in order to face the events to come.

Observe what the Gospels show us about this: "And it happened, *as He was alone praying,* that His disciples joined Him, and He asked them, saying, 'Who do the crowds say that I am?'" After hearing their answers, Jesus then asked them, "But who do you say that I am?"

To this, Simon Peter responded: "The Christ of God" (Luke 9:18–20). Or as Matthew more extensively records his words, "You are the Christ, the Son of the living God" (Matthew 16:16).

Jesus then replied, "Blessed are you, Simon Bar-Jonah, for flesh and blood has not revealed this to you, but My Father who is in heaven" (Matthew 16:17).

It was a profound, momentous confession from the

most prominent of the apostles, and it happened all because of the questions Jesus asked.

And what was Jesus doing just before this crucial conversation? Praying to the Father! "He was alone praying" (Luke 9:18). The Father had summoned Him to prayer because He wanted Jesus to know what He, the Father, had accomplished in the lives of the disciples.

In this time of prayer, the Savior received certain questions to ask the Twelve. The Father told the Son to ask them so that Jesus could witness the disciples' conviction about His identity—and having witnessed it, Jesus could then proceed to the cross: "From that time Jesus began to show to His disciples that He must go to Jerusalem, and suffer many things from the elders and chief priests and scribes, and be killed, and be raised the third day" (Matthew 16:21).

That which had been needed in the disciple's lives, and which only the Father could accomplish, was now complete, and Jesus could bring His ministry on earth to its all-important, sacrificial finish.

RECEIVING GOD'S UNDERSTANDING ABOUT OTHERS

So we see that Jesus sought the Father's direction not only for each step He took during His earthly ministry, but also to gain understanding in what was going on with the Father's activity among those whose lives He had been entrusted with. This glimpse into the dynamics of the prayer life of Jesus provides us with an important truth for our own prayer lives.

To each of us, God has entrusted other people in a variety of relationships —a marriage partner, children, co-workers, friends, and a local church family. How are you relating to them? Are you seeking the Father in prayer to understand His activity in their lives?

These people have been given by God not only to walk with you and help you carry the burdens that come with being a follower of Christ, but also so that your life can be a blessing and encouragement to them. How much time in prayer have you spent on their behalf?

As the Father reveals the people who have been entrusted to your life, are you faithfully going to God in

Little children were brought to Him that He might put His hands on them and pray.

MATTHEW 19:13

intercession that they would remain faithful? Our intercession should be as real and as urgent as the prayers of Jesus for those entrusted to Him.

As you seek God in prayer concerning those around you, God will reveal how He's working in their lives and the ways in which you can mutually work together to fulfill God's purposes in your life, family, church, community, nation, and world. Before you relate to those around you at home, at work, in your neighborhood, or in your church, be careful to spend time with the Father to receive His wisdom so that you'll be made aware of His activity in their lives.

HE STILL INTERCEDES FOR US

The role of Jesus' intercession was vital to the Father's purposes. So important was this intercession for the lives and purposes of the disciples that our Savior continues to intercede for every believer to this day.

Our resurrected Lord reigns "at the right hand of God," where He "also makes intercession for us" (Romans 8:34). The author of Hebrews says that Christ "always lives to make intercession" for "those who come to God through Him" (Hebrews 7:25); He has gone "into heaven itself… to appear in the presence of God *for us*" (Hebrews 9:24). Christ is before the Father interceding for each of us!

Jesus' strong example of intercession in His total prayer life must give us reason to think carefully through our own prayer life and that of our churches. How real, faithful, and intense is intercessory prayer in our lives? How much is being gained or lost in the lives of God's people through our praying?

Are those around you being strengthened against sin and temptation because of your prayers? This must be a major concern for all of us.

AN ALL-IMPORTANT WORD

Our continuing obligation from our Savior to pray for others is confirmed as well in the model prayer that Jesus taught His disciples.

It's important to note that the very first word of this prayer is "Our"—stressing our corporate interdependence with other believers. When the disciples first heard this prayer, little did they know how significant their lives were either to Jesus or to one another. But this all-important "Our" was designed to set their hearts not only toward God, but toward others whom God has placed around them. The same is true for us.

Likewise the repetition of that word "our" later in this prayer—in "our daily bread" and "our sins" (Luke 11:3–4) —shows again that every disciple's concern in prayer must

From Henry: God's Answers in a Son's Life

One Sunday morning as I finished preaching, I noticed a number of young men making their way to the front of the church, and they were weeping. They were responding to God's call on their lives as He had spoken through His Word during the sermon.

One of these young men was my son Tom. He wasn't usually emotional, but on that Sunday he was deeply moved.

I immediately went to Tom to see what God was saying to him. Typically for a pastor's son, he responded, "Dad, I'm okay; you need to deal with the others here who've come forward."

"Not today, Tom," I told him. "I've been praying for you for some time, and I'm the only father you have. Today I must spend time with you, and someone else can take care of the others."

Together we went back to my office, and Tom poured out his heart with many tears. God was calling him at this time to the ministry. What a glorious moment it was, as issues of a lifetime were settled between Tom and God.

Tom subsequently took a two-year overseas assignment as a student mission volunteer to Norway. He then completed seminary training and has been in full-time ministry ever since, and today serves as a senior pastor in Stravanger, Norway.

go beyond his own personal and individual interests. Each of us must remember, "I'm to pray for 'our daily bread,' not just my own needs; and I'm to look for forgiveness for 'our sins,' not just my own."

As a result of the Father's answers to Christ's intercession for His disciples, the corporate life of God's people in the early church (as seen throughout Acts and the epistles) became a vital part of the eternal purpose of God to fulfill His will for the salvation for the entire world.

Even when you're praying alone, remember that God views your life as part of the larger family of God. What He reveals to you as you pray as an individual will be connected to His purposes and activities in your family, your church, your community, your nation, and the entire world. Don't view your prayer only in isolation, but always seek to understand and connect it to the larger family of God around you.

NEEDED MORE THAN EVER

The weak condition of God's people in the churches today can be attributed to our neglect of intercession for them. This need for serious intercession from God's people is crucial in every generation, but especially ours, for there are now well over six billion living souls in our world, with their eternal destiny at stake.

From Norman: **God's Surprising Provision**

While Dana and I were in seminary, I became seriously ill from a vaccination, and I experienced great pain to the point where I couldn't use my legs and hands much of the time.

Through a relationship with a friend of the family, I was able to get into an outstanding clinic in Florida to see if they could find a solution to my medical problems. However, as seminary students, we were overwhelmed by the costs we were likely to incur. As I checked into the clinic and began taking a battery of tests, we were unsure how we would ever be able to pay for the treatment, especially since there were some difficulties with my insurance. But we knew God had created this opportunity for me to come to the clinic, and we were praying for help and needed relief.

Before I headed to the clinic for a final day of tests, the Lord impressed on our hearts to pray that before we left the doors of the clinic, God would take care of every expense there. Dana and I talked together and decided that God had indeed instructed us to pray this prayer, and that we needed to trust Him. It was a scary prayer for us, but we knew we were to pray it and to trust Him.

Later that day, as we were about to leave the clinic, I received an urgent note telling us to meet with the head of Patient Accounts. We'd been told of continuing problems with our insurance, and Dana and I were both nervous about meeting with this man.

After we went to Patient Accounts, the man we met there happened to be someone who had been at a convention with my father, and he just wanted to meet Dana and me personally. Then he told us that he had been looking over our file, and that although the clinic had recently cancelled its arrangement with our health insurance provider, for the remainder of the month they were accepting the carrier and their rate of customary charges. This meant a huge saving for us.

He also added that my account had been listed in the computer system as "Future Development" because of our friend who had referred us there, although we didn't know what this meant for us.

This man came with us when we went to check out of the clinic. A woman at the counter told us, "It's customary to pay the remainder of the bill before leaving."

We didn't know how we were going to do this, but just then the man we had met in Patient Accounts spoke up and said, "They're 'Future Development'—we're going to waive their charges."

As we walked out the clinic doors and into the heat of the Florida summer, the Lord reminded me of the prayer we had prayed that morning, and I was filled with gratefulness.

A few days after we arrived home, I received a phone call from a pastor in Florida. He told me he was the pastor of the church attended by the man we had met in Patient Accounts. He said this man had been radically impacted by the way God had answered our prayers that day. He also told us that this man was the chairman of the deacons at the church, and that his influence had affected the entire church. The pastor said he just wanted to call and thank me for how we had trusted God and prayed, because this had impacted his entire church.

We never did receive any medical solutions for my health problems that week, but God used that time to encourage His people at one of His churches. God had allowed that special time of prayer from Dana and me to bless others in the kingdom of God. We had no idea what God had in mind that day, but it taught us a whole new dimension of "Our Father" and our corporate identity with His people.

God's heart is gravely concerned about His people remaining faithful to Him as salt and light among such a needy mass of humanity. The redemption of this desperate world rests on our faithfulness to live out God's assignment.

DEALING WITH DIFFICULT PEOPLE

On this topic of praying and ministering to others, we would like to specifically address what we learn from the Savior in the way He responded to Judas Iscariot.

We noted earlier how Jesus spent all night in prayer before selecting His twelve apostles—and of course one of them was Judas Iscariot, who would later betray Him. In that all-night prayer session, we wonder if a great deal of the time was devoted to the Father's explaining to His Son this choice of Judas, and how Jesus was to relate to him. It surely must have been quite important for the Savior to know what the Father had in mind by giving Judas to Him.

When you look at the manner in which Jesus related to all the Twelve, it doesn't appear that He treated Judas any differently than the others. Yet Jesus knew in His heart that this one would ultimately betray him, and ministering to him must have been a difficult assignment for the Savior.

Through prayer, Jesus always understood how to relate to those who would oppose or persecute Him. He had

From Norman: **Praying Scripture for Others**

One of the most effective ways to pray for others in the Father's will and from the Father's agenda is to pray directly from the Scriptures.

As my wife, Dana, and I have studied the Bible and prayed, the Lord has placed a number of Scriptures on our hearts to pray for our family and those around us. We've put together a list of Scriptures that may be helpful as you pray. We encourage you to use this list—and as God places other specific Scriptures on your heart to pray for others, add those to your list as well.

For Your Marriage Partner: Colossians 3:12–24; Psalm 119:33–40; Philippians 1:9–11; 1 Corinthians 13:1–7; 1 Peter 3:8–9 (being "like-minded"; see also Luke 11:17 and 1 Corinthians 1:10); 1 John 5:18; Philippians 4:6–7.

For Your Children: Psalm 119:37; Luke 1:15; Luke 2:52 (with Proverbs 3:3–4, 1 Samuel 2:26); 1 Samuel 1:28; 1 Samuel 2:18; Psalm 8:2 (with Matthew 21:16); Isaiah 54:13; Titus 3:1–2; Proverbs 20:11; Luke 2:40; Colossians 1:9–12; Colossians 3:2; Psalm 22:9–10.

For Your Friends and Extended Family: 2 Timothy 1:7; 2 Timothy 2:15; 1 Corinthians 15:58; James 3:17–18; 1 Timothy 4:12; 1 Thessalonians 4:9–12; Matthew 6:13 (with 2 Thessalonians 3:3, James 4:7–10, and John 17:15); Numbers 6:24–26; Deuteronomy 6:5; Philippians 4:8.

For Your Pastors and Leaders: Isaiah 11:2; 1 Timothy 3:2–7, 11; 2 Chronicles 15:7; 2 Timothy 2:24–26; 1 Timothy 3:11; 1 Peter 4:11; Luke 24:45; Ephesians 3:14–4:3; Acts 14:22; Acts 18:24–25.

strong words toward many of these, such as the Pharisees. But toward Judas He continued quietly to provide every opportunity to follow Him and serve with Him. We believe the way in which Jesus related to Judas must have come from that all-night prayer when the Father instructed the Son about the Twelve (Luke 6:12–16).

What do we learn from this for our own lives?

God continues to give difficult assignments to His people, but He doesn't intend for us to move into these assignments unprepared. When God places difficult people in your life, don't simply discount them and walk away, but seek the Father and learn from Him why they have been brought into your life in God's purpose and plan. When you receive God's perspective through prayer, it will change the way you relate to those who may, in the end, not only disappoint you but oppose or betray you.

"Pray for those who spitefully use you and persecute you."

MATTHEW 5:44

When God gives you this understanding and instruction about how to treat such people, and you obey that instruction, it will bring blessing and encouragement not only to yourself but to others who are watching. And others will be watching!

From Henry: God's Perspective on Our Opponents

Throughout my ministry I've had people, for one reason or another, who not only have opposed me but who sometimes have done me harm and even caused great pain.

I've always gone to God in prayer about these persons who seemed not to have the same heart as me, but whom I knew God loved as He loved me. Over time and much waiting and listening before the Lord, God has answered and given me understanding in these circumstances.

Some of these people were later directed by God to other places. God left others as co-laborers in the work where I was serving, while reminding me that they were His and He was working in them to further develop their walk with Him. With these people I was to be present for God to use me as He chose to bring them more fully into His purposes.

In all this, God reminded me of His great mercy, grace, and love to me, and how He expected me to share with them this same grace and forgiveness I'd received from Him.

Some of those who opposed me most later needed a job reference from me. I'm so glad that my heart was kept right before the Lord, and He could show me through much prayer how my life could be used with them.

Through these times God has given me the understanding and strength to honor Him and to glorify His name, which has become a testimony to others who faced similar circumstances.

Chapter Seven

PRAYING FOR DAILY NEEDS

*J*esus taught His disciples the importance of praying for the immense issues of God's eternal kingdom. But in the model prayer He taught them, He also addressed the issue of daily needs and concerns.

At first glance, this movement in the model prayer from a focus on establishing God's kingdom and perfect will to the granting of "daily bread" presents a striking, radical change. But Jesus knew that the Father is committed to meeting His people's daily needs, and our Savior's teaching helps us recognize that our basic needs aren't met through our own efforts, but as a gift from God.

Today, as in Jesus' day, people continue to worry over life's basic necessities. The words of Jesus remain as true for us as they were for the disciples:

"Therefore do not worry, saying, 'What shall we eat?' or 'What shall we drink?' or 'What shall we wear?' For after all these things the Gentiles seek.

For your heavenly Father knows that you need all these things. But seek first the kingdom of God and His righteousness, and all these things shall be added to you." (Matthew 6:31–33)

If God tells us to pray for our everyday needs as represented in the phrase "our daily bread," then we need to understand that He also has a desire and commitment to fulfill those needs in this way. To fail to ask Him for this provision not only denies Him the opportunity to supply it, but also to receive the honor and thanksgiving for providing it.

"Ask, and it will be given to you;
    seek, and you will find;
        knock, and it will be opened to you.
For everyone who asks receives,
    and he who seeks finds,
        and to him who knocks it will be opened."
MATTHEW 7:7–8

When we come to God and ask for our daily provision, it directs our focus toward heaven, causing us to be God-centered throughout our day.

We often fail to recognize that our God is watching over us every day and cares for our most basic needs. Jesus assures us that our Father in heaven desires to "give good things *to those who ask Him*" (Matthew 7:11). God knows what you need and will provide these things as you pray in godly fear. Prayer in reverent submission opens the doors to the provision of heaven.

DAILY FORGIVENESS

Our need for forgiveness is a daily need, and this too is highlighted in the pattern for prayer that Jesus taught His disciples: "Give us day by day our daily bread. And forgive us our sins, for we also forgive everyone who is indebted to us" (Luke 11:3–4). In the same way we need forgiveness from God every day, we also must forgive those who hurt or wrong us throughout our day.

In *The Amplified Bible,* this forgiveness of others is expressed as having "let go of the debts" and having "given up resentment against our debtors." Another way to think of this is to pray, "Lord, forgive my sins in the same way I've forgiven those who sinned against me." This is a humbling thought!

From Henry: Not Knowing They Were Poor

When Marilynn and I accepted God's assignment for us to leave our church in California and for me to become the pastor of a church of ten people in Saskatoon, Saskatchewan, we used our savings to pay for our move to Canada, when there was almost no financial support or prospects of it for our family.

At this time we had four young children and were expecting our fifth. I remember praying with Marilynn and telling God that we trusted Him and knew He loved us. We accepted the challenge set before us, knowing God would provide.

We understood that there would be sacrifices as we followed our Lord. But we were concerned that our children (the oldest of whom was then only nine years old) might not understand. We knew the entire family would have to sacrifice as we lived out God's calling and willingly served Him in this pioneer setting, but we were concerned that our children might not fully understand the reason for our poverty.

This may seem a little odd, but we prayed to God to blind our children's eyes to the fact that they were being raised in a financially poor family.

We didn't tell any of the children of this prayer until they were adults. It was a surprise to us at that time to hear a testimony about this from our two sons Mel and Norman. They recounted that one day, as they were in college, they began to recount to others some of the stories of their growing up. It was at this point that both Mel and Norman realized for the first time how financially difficult the situation was in our home during their childhood.

God in His love had answered our simple prayer to protect our children in this way. And not only did He answer this prayer, but He also provided scholarships and good jobs for each of our children so they could complete their educations debt-free.

Jesus makes two important points with this statement on forgiveness. First, He understood our great need to be forgiven. Second, He understood the danger in the believer's life of unforgiveness toward others.

> *Then Jesus said, "Father, forgive them,*
> *for they do not know what they do."*
> LUKE 23:34

This lesson that the Lord teaches about forgiveness is often the most difficult for us to practice and probably one of the most common hindrances to our prayer life. But the issue of forgiveness is so vital that Jesus continued to expand on it after teaching His disciples the model prayer: "For if you forgive men their trespasses, your heavenly Father will also forgive you. But if you do not forgive men their trespasses, neither will your Father forgive your trespasses" (Matthew 6:14–15).

On another occasion the Savior stated, "Whenever you stand praying, if you have anything against anyone, forgive him, that your Father in heaven may also forgive you your trespasses" (Mark 11:25). There is a vital connection between prayer and forgiveness!

God's forgiveness towards us in our daily lives depends on our willingness to extend forgiveness to others. This doesn't mean God has created a tally sheet to see if He can extend forgiveness to you. Rather, it means that anyone who has received God's forgiveness and is truly walking closely with the Father will also extend forgiveness toward others.

Not only does unforgiveness hinder our fellowship with others and with God, but it distracts us during our praying. Unforgiveness and grudges will occupy a person's mind and thoughts, causing that person to lose the needed sensitivity and concentration to focus on the heavenly Father during prayer. Jesus was teaching the disciples to not allow any part of unforgiveness to hinder their prayers to the Father…as an inherent part of their looking to Him to meet all their daily needs.

Jesus continued to stress this truth about forgiveness throughout His ministry, as witnessed in His parable of the unforgiving servant (Matthew 18:21–35). For us to hold unforgiveness in our hearts towards others is sin, and this sin will inescapably hinder our prayer lives. If you're out of fellowship with God due to this sin of unforgiveness, you'll not be able to pray effectively.

Chapter Eight

THE CERTAINTY OF GOD'S ANSWERS

nother profound distinctive of the prayer life of Jesus that we must examine further is His certainty and full experience of the Father's answers to His prayers.

As Jesus sought to understand unmistakably the Father's will, the Father laid His heart over the Son's heart and mind. In His unceasing love for the Son, the Father in His faithfulness always revealed His will to Him in answer to His prayers.

Jesus described this relationship in these words: "The Father loves the Son, and shows Him all things that He Himself does" (John 5:20). Prayer always brought Jesus into oneness with the Father and His will.

HE WAS HEARD…AND HE WAS ANSWERED

After reading in Hebrews how Jesus, in the days of His flesh, diligently prayed to the Father with loud cries and tears, we encounter the simple yet profound statement that He "was heard" (Hebrews 5:7). All prayer by the Son was heard by the Father, as is all prayer from all of His children. Jesus knew the Father, and was assured of this truth. When you look at the life of Jesus you see an absolute trust and confidence that His prayers were not only heard, but answered.

"Therefore I say to you,
whatever things you ask when you pray,
believe that you receive them,
and you will have them."
MARK 11:24

We see this assurance on the occasion when the Savior prayed and prepared to feed a vast multitude with only five loaves and two fish. Jesus simply "took the five loaves and the two fish, and *looking up to heaven,* He blessed and broke them, and gave them to the disciples to set before the multitude" (Luke 9:16).

Another powerful illustration of Christ's confidence

that He was heard by the Father is the moment when He prepared to raise Lazarus from the dead. "Jesus lifted up His eyes and said, 'Father, I thank You that You have heard Me. And I know that You always hear Me, but because of the people who are standing by I said this, that they may believe that You sent Me'" (John 11:41–42).

Jesus could make this statement because He was in constant prayer to the Father, and He knew by experience that the Father always listened and answered. What a testimony to each of us today!

Have we cultivated a prayer life in which we can say along with Christ, "Father, I know that You always hear me"?

This great truth concerning prayer—that God always hears His children when they pray—is expressed in the description of God in Hebrews 11:6: "He is a rewarder of those who diligently seek Him." Have you consistently sought God in prayer believing that He hears and that He will reward your diligence to know Him?

POWER FROM THE SPIRIT, IN ANSWER TO PRAYER

Because of the certainty of God's answers to His prayers, Jesus' life was characterized by the empowerment of the Spirit. The early church—which understood the importance of prayer in the life and ministry of the Lord—experienced this Spirit-empowerment as well.

From the witness of the book of Acts we learn that the early believers obeyed their command from Jesus to wait for the Spirit's coming (Luke 24:49; Acts 1:4). While they waited, they followed their Lord's example of crying out to the Father. Scripture says that during this time they "all continued with one accord in prayer and supplication" (Acts 1:14).

In light of Jesus' promise, the Scriptures also record God's answer to their crying out in prayer, as the band of believers gathered on the day of Pentecost: "And suddenly there came a sound from heaven, as of a rushing mighty wind, and it filled the whole house where they were sitting.... And they were all filled with the Holy Spirit" (Acts 2:2–4).

Throughout the pages of Acts we see the believers seeking God in prayer during times of crisis, and praying for boldness in the face of opposition. And again we see God's answers and the Spirit's empowerment: "And when they had prayed, the place where they were assembled together was shaken; and they were all filled with the Holy Spirit, and they spoke the word of God with boldness" (Acts 4:31). Filled with the Spirit, they proceeded to let

God use their lives to turn the Roman Empire upside down.

What about our lives as Christians today? What about our churches? Have we followed the example of Christ and received God's answers and the Spirit's empowerment as a result?

The Spirit is waiting and watching today to bring power and enablement—in answer to prayer—to those who will submit their lives to God with a heart set to obey. This is the kind of person the Spirit desires to strengthen to accomplish the will of God.

LETTING OTHERS KNOW OF GOD'S ANSWERS

Prayer with the Father is an exciting time as He reveals His heart and direction for your life.

Once the Father has unfolded His will for the next step ahead of you, it's a natural response to want to share with others what you've learned. However, when we tell others what we now know from our time alone with God, those around us will often fail to understand it or to receive it favorably.

When that happens to you—simply be faithful to obey all that the Lord has commanded.

We've seen that God can be counted on to hear and answer our prayer. But what about when His answer is no?

Let's look again at the prayer of Jesus in Gethsemane. Jesus specifically prayed, "Abba, Father, all things are possible for You. *Take this cup away from Me*" (Mark 14:36).

Did God answer this prayer?

He did, and His answer was no. The Father would not be taking away this cup from His Son.

The Savior was heard by the Father, and His prayer was answered by the Father, but in Gethsemane that answer was no. Jesus was loved by His Father and continued to submit His life to the Father's will, but concerning the removal of the cross, the removal of the burden of the sins of the world, the removal of His death—the answer was no.

Receiving this answer, Jesus rose from prayer in the garden and stepped forward, without wavering, into the assignment He had been given by the Father.

How do you respond to God when His answer is no? When you make your request and God doesn't grant it, do you continue to argue with Him to try and get your way?

When you come before God in prayer, remember whose Presence you have entered. He is God, and you are not. We can make our request—but the outcome is completely up to Him.

When God's answer is no, it doesn't mean you haven't been heard by the Father, or that He doesn't understand or care. His answer comes from perfect love and understanding. He must answer no to some of our requests because He has perfect knowledge of our situation and of our future as well, while we do not. For some of our requests, answering yes would take us out of His plan for our lives.

So when God's answer comes and that answer is no, follow the example of our Lord, and say, "Not my will, but Yours, be done."

Jesus was not delivered from the cross after His prayer in Gethsemane, but He was delivered from the grave by His resurrection. His prayer *was* answered—as God intended. Jesus won a victory over sin and death in His resurrection, and Scripture was fulfilled: "Death is swallowed up in victory." Therefore we can say with Paul, "O Death, where is your sting? O Hades, where is your victory? The sting of death is sin, and the strength of sin is the law. But thanks be to God, who gives us the victory through our Lord Jesus Christ" (1 Corinthians 15:54–57).

Even if God's answer is no when we cry out to Him in our weakness and need, we can take comfort from the experience of Christ in Gethsemane. He had entered the garden saying, "My soul is exceedingly sorrowful, even to death" (Mark 14:34), but as He prayed, "an angel appeared to Him from heaven, strengthening Him" (Luke 22:43).

Our God is faithful to bring provision to all who call upon Him, and in our Savior's near-death experience in prayer, God brought a ministering angel to strengthen Him in His resolve to do His Father's will.

"If you then, being evil, know how to give good gifts to your children, how much more will your Father who is in heaven give good things to those who ask Him!"

MATTHEW 7:11

When we seek after God, He always accompanies our weakness with His strengthening provision.

This was certainly true in the life of Paul, who pleaded

three times for the Lord to remove his "thorn of the flesh," but God's answer was no. What God gave Paul instead was a greater awareness and experience of God's grace and strength: "And He said to me, 'My grace is sufficient for you, for My strength is made perfect in weakness.'... Therefore I take pleasure in infirmities, in reproaches, in needs, in persecutions, in distresses, for Christ's sake. For when I am weak, then I am strong" (2 Corinthians 12:7–10).

So often God allows us to understand and experience and appreciate His grace most when something we want and pray for is not granted us—all because of His perfect love and wisdom.

God will always come to the one who continues to submit in prayer to His will and doesn't lose heart. The provisions of God are many, and can come in a multitude of ways.

From Norman: Getting God's Perspective

Dana and I minister alongside my parents in Blackaby Ministries International. The work is particularly demanding and abundant at times, and because of the small number of people in the ministry, we're often very tired.

Recently, as we were obeying God's direction, we faced some hard and hurtful opposition. The opposition was very strong and continuing, to the point that Dana and I began to become discouraged. However we were determined not to lose heart, but to continue seeking God for direction and strength.

During my wife's prayer time, the Lord impressed this upon her: "Dana, don't worry about what others say or how they oppose the work. Ask Me what I think of you and of Norman, and whether I've called you to this assignment." Dana told me about this, and we began that day to ask in prayer, "God, what *do* You think about us and the work we have been doing in this assignment?"

While He did not send an angel to strengthen us, as He did with Jesus in Gethsemane, He did do something very special. Within a two-day period, five unrelated people from different places called or emailed us to tell us that God had impressed upon their hearts to let us know how thankful they were for us, and how the work we were doing had been a blessing to their lives.

You can imagine what that did for our hearts. It strengthened us, confirmed what we were doing, and most of all, communicated our Father's approval.

Chapter Nine

PROTECTION FROM TEMPTATION

*T*hrough prayer, Jesus not only came to know the Father's will, but fully prepared Himself to continue obeying it—and to resist any temptation that would stand in the way of completing His assignment from the Father.

The book of Hebrews states that our Lord was "in all points tempted as we are, yet without sin" (Hebrews 4:15). Jesus was tempted not just in some points, but in *all*. Yet He found strength from the Father to resist every temptation and to stay on the path of obedience.

Closeness to the Father in prayer was the key to keeping Him from temptation, and this can be our experience as well.

EVERY REASON TO PRAY

Jesus taught His disciples that they "always ought to pray and not lose heart" (Luke 18:1). Or as *The Amplified Bible* expresses it, "They ought always to pray and not to turn coward (faint, lose heart, and give up)."

Jesus taught them this because He knew the provision of God—He knew by experience that the Father in heaven was always faithful to those who continued to pray and who did not lose heart, and the Father would always give strength against temptation to those who truly trusted Him in this.

We learn this in a pronounced way as Jesus entered Gethsemane. His overriding message to His disciples at this moment was a simple and urgent exhortation to pray for protection against temptation: "Watch and pray, lest you enter into temptation. The spirit indeed is willing, but the flesh is weak" (Mark 14:38). He was making clear the role of prayer in dealing with temptation. The One who knew and successfully dealt with temptation was telling them how to guard themselves from stumbling.

All of you must keep awake
(give strict attention, be cautious and active)
and watch and pray, that you may not come
into temptation.
The spirit indeed is willing.
but the flesh is weak.
MATTHEW 26:41 AMP

Temptation and testing awaited all the disciples very soon, and Jesus knew that only by watching and praying could they avoid spiritual disaster. Not only was it important for Jesus Himself to be in prayer during His time in Gethsemane, but their praying with Him would also provide the spiritual alertness and preparation for the temptations they themselves were about to face.

Jesus was clearly aware of the particular difficulties Peter was about to encounter, as we see in what He spoke to Peter earlier that evening: "Simon, Simon! Indeed, Satan has asked for you, that he may sift you as wheat" (Luke 22:31); and especially these words: "Most assuredly, I say to you, the rooster shall not crow till you have denied Me three times" (John 13:38). Knowing that Peter's understanding of His own intimate prayer fellowship would be crucial for the trials he would soon experience, Jesus took Peter, along with James and John, and went further into the garden to pray.

FIGHTING SORROW AND SLEEP

Jesus instructed these three, then stepped a little beyond them to pray alone. Scripture doesn't record why Jesus later interrupted His praying to go back and speak with the disciples. He may have wanted to tell them that the issue of their eternal salvation had been settled. He had submitted

His will to the Father's will, and was now going to the cross to carry their sin and make eternal life possible for them.

But when He returned to them, He did not find them watching and praying as He had commanded, but sleeping. Jesus came back to the disciples three times, and not once were they awake.

Luke tells us that they were "sleeping from sorrow" (Luke 22:45). While the sorrow is not explained, the many words Jesus had spoken earlier that evening about the suffering and trials to come (see Luke 22:14–22, 31–34; John 13:21, 38; 14:28; 15:19–20; 16:1–2, 6, 16–20) might have been the reason for their sorrow.

> *Keep awake and watch and pray [constantly],*
> *that you may not enter into temptation;*
> *the spirit indeed is willing, but the flesh is weak.*
> MARK 14:38 AMP

We don't know everything that concerned and burdened the disciples at this time, but each of us knows how tension and trouble can sap our strength. The disciples were tired and physically unable to remain awake at such an important time in their lives and in human history.

However, the same God who strengthened Jesus as He prayed—and sent an angel to minister to Him—could also have strengthened the disciples during this time if they had chosen to obey their Master and stay awake to watch and pray. The resources of God are available to the person who prays!

Sleeping, the disciples never knew what could have happened if only they had obeyed their Lord and watched and prayed with alertness. They might have started to understand what was happening at this moment in history, in a way that only Jesus and the Father understood it. Had they stayed awake, the disciples could have experienced God's provision to keep them from entering into temptation, and perhaps they themselves might have been ministered to by an angel.

THE LORD WANTS TO PREPARE YOU

We must apply this lesson to our lives as well. Does Jesus know what we're about to encounter? Does He know what temptations we're about to experience? Yes, He does. And He wants to prepare us for them in advance through our relationship with Him in prayer.

Be very sensitive to the Lord when He calls you to go further with Him in prayer. In such times, expect Him to reveal to you more of Himself, more of His purposes, and more of His will. In addition, He will prepare you for any coming events that will test your faith.

Never forget that God will also be faithful to come to your life as you seek after Him in prayer, and don't lose heart. He may not send an angel to minister to you, but He'll come and strengthen you, bringing victory through your life and thus accomplishing His will.

TO GUARD AGAINST STUMBLING

Praying to be protected during temptation is not simply for the times when you're struggling with sin and cry out for God's help. This should be something we pray for in advance.

On the night before Jesus died, after He had taught His disciples so many powerful truths as recorded in chapters 13 through 15 of John, He made this incredible statement: "These things I have spoken to you, *that you should not be made to stumble*" (John 16:1). He gave the disciples these words of truth so they would not stumble in all that awaited them.

In the same way, He waits to instruct you for all that awaits you—if you'll come to Him in prayer.

This emphasis from Jesus on using prayer to guard against temptation is reinforced in the pattern of prayer that He taught His disciples. The closing words of this model prayer are these: "And do not lead us into temptation, but deliver us from the evil one" (Luke 11:4).

Every day we're faced with temptation. There's no end to the types of temptation Christians face, as our sin nature rises up and demands our own interests and our own way of thinking as opposed to God's ways and thinking.

He said to them, Pray that you may not [at all] enter into temptation.

LUKE 22:40 AMP

Whenever we sin against God, we place our desires and thinking above God's instruction. We're no longer serving God or fulfilling His will for our lives. How do we protect against this? Through prayer to our Father.

When you consider the struggles with temptation and sin in your own life, what role are you allowing prayer to play in this battle? How much time and energy are you willing to devote in prayer in order to receive victory over sin in your life?

In His great high priestly prayer in John 17, Jesus made this request for His followers: "I do not pray that You should take them out of the world, but that You should keep them from the evil one" (John 17:15). We're to remain in this world as His witnesses, but this will bring trials and difficult challenges into our lives. The enemy is real and desires to destroy our effectiveness as Christians. Therefore, Jesus instructed and encouraged all His disciples to pray for the Father's protection.

TO GUARD AGAINST FALLING AWAY

Over the years, we've encountered many people who started off following after the Lord, but eventually fell to the wayside because they were unprepared for the temptations they would face while pursuing the assignments God had given.

Therefore in our prayers we need to be asking the Father to keep us from stumbling in temptation and for deliverance from evil. This doesn't mean we instantly gain some kind of automatic protection against falling away. But by regularly going to the Father and asking for His protection, we'll greatly strengthen our lives against failing the test or stumbling in our daily walk with God.

The Savior's words in the garden—"Pray that you may not enter into temptation" (Luke 22:40)—are needed today more than ever. Are you protecting yourself, your family, and your church from falling into temptation through active prayer to the Father? If you aren't, then don't be surprised if you're overtaken by sin.

Chapter Ten

OBEYING WHAT WE LEARN
IN PRAYER

*O*ur Savior's entire life was patterned by daily adjustments to the Father's will. As Jesus expressed it in John 8:29, "I always do those things that please Him." For Jesus, obedience was an absolute, and it must be for us as well.

Every time Jesus entered His Father's presence, the Son's understanding was opened to what the Father was doing. Having thus learned God's agenda through prayer, and having thoroughly prepared Himself through prayer for each assignment awaiting Him, our Savior's consistent example was then to immediately follow His Father's revealed will by fully adjusting His life to the Father's purposes.

This pattern was the heart of Jesus' decisions in every aspect of His behavior. Jesus always knew what to do and say because the Father had instructed Him through their intimate relationship of prayer, and the Son faithfully adhered to all the Father's instructions.

A COMMITMENT TO ACCOUNTABILITY

In the days of His flesh, the same godly fear and reverent submission that characterized our Lord's attitude in prayer also characterized every aspect of the way He lived.

There were many times during His public ministry when Jesus could have gone against the Father's will and provided comfort for Himself or avoided pain. He acknowledged this fact when the soldiers came to arrest Him in Gethsemane. "Do you think," He asked them, "that I cannot now pray to My Father, and He will provide Me with more than twelve legions of angels?" Then He made clear that He would not do this because He was committed to God's revealed will: "How then could the Scriptures be fulfilled, that it must happen thus?" (Matthew 26:53–54).

He rose up from prayer...

LUKE 22:45

The necessity of obedience and accountability was a driving force in His life. At so many points in His ministry, Jesus could have avoided the difficult road ahead. Instead, the deep sense of accountability that fully marked the prayers of Jesus fully marked His life as well. Once He heard from the Father in prayer, He lived out His life with a determined purpose to obey everything God set before Him.

This sense of awesome accountability intensified as He approached the cross. He knew His death was His Father's will, and He desired to be faithful and to give an account to the Father. Jesus kept this sense of accountability to the very end. On the night before His death, He was able to say to the Father, "I have finished the work which You have given Me to do" (John 17:4). And on the cross itself He said in a loud cry to the Father, "It is finished!" (John 19:30).

LIVING OUT GOD'S AGENDA

God's Word shows us that even at the young age of twelve, Jesus was keenly aware of following His heavenly Father's agenda. In response to His parents' frantic search for Him, which finally ended when they found Him in the Temple, He asked them, "Why did you seek Me? Did you not know that I must be about My Father's business?" (Luke

2:49). From an early age, Jesus was following His Father's agenda, and the Father's will always came first!

This commitment guided His entire life. Decades later, when ministry crowds pressed around Jesus so that He and the disciples "were not even able to eat," the family of Jesus "heard about this" and "went to take charge of him" (Mark 3:20–21 NIV). But Jesus again made it clear that His Father's will and work came first (see Mark 3:32–35).

JESUS LEARNED OBEDIENCE

This obedience to the Father's will was not something merely automatic or mechanical for Jesus. It was instead vitally linked with the Son's continuing fellowship with the Father, a relationship marked by the Son's active dependence on the Father—as well as by His continued *learning*.

Returning again to the summary in Hebrews 5 of Jesus' prayer life in the days of His flesh, we find an extraordinary statement. After being told how the Son prayed so constantly and passionately and was heard because of His reverent submission, we read this: "Though He was a Son, yet He *learned obedience* by the things which He suffered" (Hebrews 5:8). Even the Son of God "learned obedience"—and He did so by suffering.

This passage earlier emphasized Christ's humanity with the phrase "in the days of His flesh," which provides great encouragement for us as we pray. Then it points to His deity as the "Son," yet it again emphasizes something the Savior experienced which all human beings also share—and that is suffering.

Although the Father's answer to His prayers clearly involved hardship, Jesus never quit praying or obeying. It was precisely in His afflictions that Jesus "learned" obedience in the sense of personally and practically taking hold of every aspect of obedience in every situation that awaited Him.

Jesus' suffering was real, but through prayer, He knew its purpose in the will of God was to provide salvation for all mankind.

His example is also the pattern for us, as we learn and practice obedience even in the most difficult things that God brings us as part of His agenda. Obedience is about learning. As we pray, we can know and expect God to teach and transform us in order to conform us to His will, and the suffering He purposes for us will be a key ingredient in this.

OUR OWN OPPORTUNITIES
TO LEARN OBEDIENCE

It's often at the moment of suffering that people stop seeking after God through prayer. But in light of our Lord's example, we should see suffering not as discouraging but as an opportunity to make further progress in obedience.

And the only way we'll know how to learn from our difficult times is through a vital prayer life. If we remain in communication with God through prayer, God can grant us understanding and strength during our suffering.

When God takes you into a time of affliction, remember that this was the method the Father used to teach the Son obedience, resulting in reverent submission to the pur-

He said, "Father, into Your hands

I commit My spirit."

LUKE 23:46

poses of God. Prayer brought Jesus into the Father's will even when it hurt.

WHEN WE FACE PAIN AND LOSS

Our difficulties in the Christian life usually have less to do with trying to understand what God's will is, and more to do with simply obeying the instructions God has already expressed—especially when these instructions point us toward trouble and trials.

The receiving and accepting of our God-given assignments are settled in prayer, but when God reveals His will, it can require real hardships in the life of the one who is following after Christ. It will often include much pain, especially at the front end of the assignment. It may require giving up family and friends, homeland, income, reputation, influence, and many other things.

At these points, the prayer life of Jesus is our pattern and encouragement. Don't suppose that because you're following God's direction that it will always be easy to accept, obey, and live out the assignment. There's a cost to following after Christ that's real and often painful. To feel the weight of this cost is not a rejection of the assignment, nor is it a sign of wavering faith. It is simply an opportunity to learn obedience through suffering, as Christ did.

Today, are you shrinking from this measure of praying?

From Henry: **A Difficult Separation**

When I was seventeen, God clearly placed His hand upon me and asked that I be exclusively His for the rest of my life.

After university, I was faced with a difficult choice. God had called me into His service and I knew I needed seminary training. However, my parents were not young when I was born, and by this time they were in the later years of life. I wanted so much to spend quality time with them as an adult, but now I felt I must leave them in my native British Columbia and go to California to attend seminary.

As I prepared to leave, one night I walked out under the stars and cried, knowing that my parents might die while I was away. But they had told me that the greatest joy and honor to them was for me to be in the center of God's will.

In prayer, God gave me not only the understanding of His call on my life but the needed preparation and foundation to continue in the assignment in the face of difficult circumstances.

While I was in seminary, my father did die, and about three years later my mother passed away as well. However, years earlier in prayer I'd already "settled" with God the fact that this would likely happen. I loved my parents and missed them, but I knew that my life had meaning and purpose only as I exclusively followed my Lord. In my grief, God sustained me with the knowledge that I'll be able to spend eternity with my parents.

Maybe you've gone before the Lord and He gave you an assignment. Now that you know what He's asking, deep prayers and supplications will need to pour out from your heart to the One who is able to do all things. The *strength* to continue stepping out in obedience will come through prayer to the Father.

DEPENDING ON THE FATHER'S INTERVENTION

As Jesus understood the plan of God for His life, He also recognized that apart from the guidance and strength of the Father He would not have been able to carry out the task. Jesus understood His need for constant "intervention" from the Holy Spirit, and His life from the very beginning demonstrated His dependence on the Spirit.

Therefore the consistent witness we see from Christ's life is one of empowerment through dependence upon the mighty Spirit of God.

Jesus also prayed for the Father to send the Spirit to dwell with and empower His disciples: "I will pray the Father, and He will give you another Helper, that He may abide with you forever—the Spirit of truth... you know Him, for He dwells with you and will be in you" (John 14:16–17).

He gave His disciples this promise regarding the Spirit: "He will teach you all things, and bring to your remembrance all things that I said to you" (John 14:26). He spoke of the Holy Spirit as their "Helper" and "the Spirit of truth," and added, "He will testify of Me" (John 15:26).

After His resurrection, Jesus promised the disciples that they would be "endued with power from on high" (Luke 24:49), and just before He ascended to heaven He told them, "But you shall receive power when the Holy Spirit has come upon you; and you shall be witnesses to Me in Jerusalem, and in all Judea and Samaria, and to the end of the earth" (Acts 1:8). For empowering their lives to fulfill God's will, the disciples were to wait for the same enabling Spirit who had descended upon Christ.

Jesus cried out with a loud voice, saying...

"My God, My God..."

MATTHEW 27:46

This dependence upon the Spirit of God must be a pattern for our lives as well. The words of our Lord in John 15:5 (NIV)—"Apart from Me you can do nothing"— are true for us today. When God reveals His plans for your life there ought to be deep agonizing prayer flowing from your life because of your understanding that without

Him, you absolutely cannot accomplish His assignment.

If the Father has revealed His will and the manner in which He desires to use you, do you sense an urgent need for the Father's "intervention" on your behalf through the Spirit?

God desires that we be witness of Him in this world, and we must be empowered for it. Have you gone alone with God, as well as joined others in prayer, to receive "power from on high" in order to gain strength, understanding, and direction to live out God's will?

WHEN OTHERS DON'T UNDERSTAND

As Jesus was faithful to live out obedience to the Father's agenda, His disciples often didn't understand what He was doing, and He had to firmly rebuke them and reorient them to His involvement with the Father's activities.

The most prominent occasion of this was when Peter actually "took Him aside and began to rebuke Him" after Jesus had told the disciples that He must go to Jerusalem, be killed, and be raised again the third day (Matthew 16:21–22). Jesus had to tell Peter, "Get behind Me, Satan! You are an offense to Me, for you are not mindful of the things of God, but the things of men" (16:23).

Christ's example was that regardless of others' reactions, He continued to obey what He had learned from God in prayer.

From Henry: When Others Think We're Mistaken

More than forty years ago, Marilynn and I sensed a call to foreign missions. We applied to serve in Africa and were set to go, but at the last minute one of our sons started having seizures. We were turned down at the mission board because of this medical problem.

Shortly after this we were called to leave the Los Angeles area to pastor a small church in Saskatoon, Saskatchewan. Many people tried to convince us that we hadn't heard correctly from the Lord. It didn't make sense to them that we would leave a thriving ministry in Southern California to go to a church of only ten people in the Canadian prairies. Many of the people close to us were convinced we were making a mistake.

We also had to grapple with the fact that we had felt such a strong call to foreign missions, and yet I was retuning to my native land.

However, in obedience we followed the Lord to Saskatoon.

In time, a mission to foreign nations did indeed become a huge part of God's assignment for us. Today, Marilynn and I travel the world speaking and leading conferences. As I prepare this book for print, I'm in

Mexico, and this will be followed by a ministry trip to England, followed by two weeks of service in South Africa and Mozambique.

Because we obeyed the Lord when He spoke to us four decades ago, even when those around us didn't understand, we've been able to join God in ministry in over a hundred countries around the globe.

Over the years, as I sought the Father's will in ministry and later shared with fellow pastors and church leaders the things God had revealed to me as I prayed, there have been many times when these pastors and leaders would not accept these things. I found, however, that it wasn't my place to convince or argue, but simply to be obedient to the Lord's words.

Now, after so many years of ministry, I can say that the Lord has always been faithful to bring about everything He has said to me as I sought Him in prayer.

Chapter Eleven

GOD'S WILL ACCOMPLISHED

From our Savior's times of prayer with the Father, followed by His obedience to the Father's will as revealed in those times, Jesus did not fail in anything God gave Him to do. Because He always listened to His Father's agenda and was always obedient, the Father was free to fully accomplish His eternal purposes through the Son.

STAYING TRUE TO THE FATHER'S ETERNAL PLAN

Jesus knew the Father had eternity in mind each time He prayed. This was supremely revealed at the most critical moment for the accomplishment of the Father's will through the Son—on the night of His prayer in Gethsemane. When Jesus said, "Not My will, but Yours, be done" (Luke 22:42), all was now settled, and God's great salvation for the world would begin to unfold. Eternity was now to be gloriously affected.

In many ways, Gethsemane was the *Father's* moment. He had eternally planned and purposed salvation, and had worked throughout history to bring everything to this point. If Jesus had not come to this in reverent submission, God's eternal plan to redeem the world would have been lost.

God waited…and Jesus, in godly fear, submitted, making certain God's eternal plan for our great salvation.

This was the climax of our Savior's driving motivation in His life, a motivation He had so often made clear:

My food is to do the will of Him who sent Me, and to finish His work. (John 4:34)

I do not seek My own will but the will of the Father who sent Me. (John 5:30)

I have come down from heaven, not to do My own will, but the will of Him who sent Me. (John 6:38)

His never-wavering commitment to God's plan and purpose is the reason He could say to the Father at the end of His ministry, "I have finished the work which You have given Me to do" (John 17:4), and to cry out from the cross, "It is finished!" (John 19:30).

Let's return one last time to the passage in Hebrews that shows us the essence of Christ's prayer life in the days of His flesh. After showing us His constant and passionate prayers, and that His prayers were heard because of His reverent submission, and that Jesus then learned obedience by the things He suffered, the passage then concludes with this statement about the Savior: "And having been perfected, He became the author of eternal salvation to all who obey Him" (Hebrews 5:9).

Through this all-consuming process of continual prayer, submission, and obedience in the midst of suffering, Jesus was *made perfect*.

For the Father to accomplish His plan for the world's redemption, there had to be a perfect and complete sacrifice for sin. Jesus, in His prayerful submission to His Father, was *made* complete by the Father. Prayer in the Son's life gave the Father the opportunity to shape Jesus to be His perfect and acceptable sacrifice for sin. This was the Father's activity in the total prayer life of Jesus, and the redemption of the world depended on it.

In the same way, prayer in our lives is purposed by God to change and shape us to His will and purpose so He can accomplish His redemptive will through us.

The redemption of the world now rests on this activity

of God in *us,* as a result of our prayers, while the Father works to perfect us and shape us into the image of His Son. Our immediate and full submission, even when it costs us greatly, is the Father's purpose for our individual lives, for our families, and for our churches, that the world may come to know and experience God's great salvation.

GREATER WORKS THAN THE WORKS OF JESUS

Because of Jesus' prayer life and obedience to what He learned, a watching world came to know and experience the wonders and truths of the Father. Jesus could proclaim, "He who has seen Me has seen the Father" and "the Father who dwells in Me does the works" (John 14:9–10).

When He spoke those words, Jesus then went on to make this surprising statement to His disciples: "Most assuredly, I say to you, he who believes in Me, the works that I do he will do also; and *greater works than these he will do,* because I go to My Father" (John 14:12). God's intention was for the disciples to do even "greater works" in their lives than the Savior Himself had done.

Jesus then carefully linked the accomplishment of these "greater works" to the disciples' prayer life: "And whatever you *ask in My name,* that I will do, that the Father may be glorified in the Son. If you *ask anything in My name,* I will do it" (John 14:13–14).

> Then He said to them,
>   "The harvest truly is great,
> but the laborers are few; therefore pray the Lord
>   of the harvest to send out laborers
> into His harvest."

LUKE 10:2

As the Father heard and answered Jesus when He prayed, so Jesus would answer His disciples when they prayed, and in so doing, God would be glorified.

This is God's intention for us as well. In a day in which there is much prayer, are we therefore also seeing such "greater works" as a result of those prayers?

SO MUCH AT STAKE

So much is at stake through our prayer life!

Worldwide revival waits on the reverent, submissive prayer of God's people, in the same way that Christ submitted His life to the Father's will and, in turn, was the instrument used to bring salvation. As we submit our lives to the Father's will, He can then use our lives to touch a lost and hurting world.

Prayer adjusted Jesus fully to the Father's will, and God's great salvation was purchased. This must be the clear and simple pattern for our lives. May we also let God adjust us as we pray and secure eternal salvation for the entire world, according to the Father's will. Then our lives will be of maximum use to bring healing and repentance to the church and salvation to the lost world.

So often we fail to recognize that the Father's will for our lives also impacts eternity. Each day, however, we come in contact with Christians who need a fresh word from the Lord, while we also encounter many who don't know Christ and need to hear and see the gospel witnessed through our lives. If you're a child of God, then your life, as used by the Father, will affect eternity for those around you.

CHANGING THE WORLD

What kind of person does God use to change the course of history? He uses those to whom He can entrust the deepest things of His heart *through prayer.* Prayer releases our lives to the Father and gives Him unhindered access to use us to accomplish His will.

This is really the pattern of God's nature, His ways, His purposes, and His activities through the entire Bible. He sets the pace, then chooses and calls someone to walk with

Him so He can complete His purposes through them. They know by prayer what God's will is for their lives, and as they obey Him, He accomplishes that will through them. In turn, their world and their generation are eternally affected.

This kind of prayer life releases an individual to the will of the Father, so Almighty God can use such a person in His purpose of drawing people to Himself in this hurting and confused world.

God desires to shape the prayer lives of His people so Christians can know with confidence that they've sought the Father's will and are walking in it. God desires that His people spend enough time with Him so they can say with confidence that the words they share with the surrounding world are from the heart of God and not merely from man. God desires to have a people who are convinced through prayer that God is in control, that His ways are right, and that their hearts' desire is to immediately obey His direction found in deep, life-changing prayer.

To continue in this kind of prayer, followed by absolute obedience to the will of God, will then result in our hearing these words from the Master: "Well done, good and faithful servant" (Matthew 25:21).

Chapter Twelve

FOR THE GLORY OF GOD

In His praying, as well as in every aspect of life, Jesus was consciously seeking the glory of His Father. That is why He could say at the end of His ministry, "I have glorified You on the earth" (John 17:4).

ALLOWING OTHERS TO GLORIFY GOD

When people witnessed the life of Christ, they were witnessing the *Father*—and they glorified Him. When God the Father worked through His Son to heal a paralytic, Scripture records this response: "Now when the multitudes saw it, they marveled and *glorified God,* who had given such power to men" (Matthew 9:8).

When "great multitudes" followed Him up a mountain above the Sea of Galilee, and there He healed "the lame, blind, mute, maimed, and many others," this was the people's reaction: "The multitude marveled when they saw the mute speaking, the maimed made whole, the lame walking, and the blind seeing; and *they glorified the God of Israel"* (Matthew 15:29–31).

When Jesus raised a widow's son from the dead, what happened next among the people was remarkable: "Then fear came upon all, and they *glorified God,* saying… 'God has visited His people'" (Luke 7:16).

"Father, glorify Your name."

JOHN 12:28

Every miracle God did through Jesus revealed some aspect of the nature of God to the surrounding people. Through Christ's life they experienced God—and they therefore glorified God, knowing He was present among them.

The Father was able to express His love to the people through the Son because He was (and continues to be) a God of wonders, power, and might. Through Jesus, He healed the blind, the lame, and the lepers. He fed multitudes, stilled the storms, raised the dead, and—most important of all—forgave and healed the sinner.

All this was just what God the Father had planned from eternity. In all this, He was being glorified by Jesus. And all this was what Jesus had in mind as He said to His Father, "I have glorified You on the earth" (John 17:4).

Jesus was the chosen instrument through whom the Father was able to make Himself known to mankind, so we can experience Him fully. We can come to know His nature (full of love), His ways (present, personal, real, and active among us), His purposes (redemption for His people, and His presence moving through us so all the world can be blessed through us).

THE FULLNESS OF GOD'S PRESENCE

The glory of God is related to the fullness of God's presence and activity, which was so very real and observable in Christ.

As the Savior interceded for His disciples, He acknowledged that He had given them "the glory which You gave Me," and all for this reason: "that they may be one just as We are one" (John 17:22). He was asking for the Father's full affirmation of His life and presence with His disciples, knowing that this would be for the accomplishment of His loving, eternal purposes—"that the world may know that

You have sent Me, and have loved them as You have loved Me" (John 17:23).

This same fullness of the Father's presence is what God desires all of His children to experience—to "be filled with all the fullness of God," as Paul expressed it, and all for the Father's glory: "To Him be glory in the church by Christ Jesus to all generations, forever and ever" (Ephesians 3:19–21).

As He prayed,

the appearance of His face was altered.

LUKE 9:29

HOW WE CAN BRING GOD GLORY

Jesus taught His disciples that their prayer life would also glorify God. The Son continually tied prayer and glorifying the Father together. He stated, "Whatever you ask in My name, that I will do, that *the Father may be glorified* in the Son" (John 14:13). And again: "If you abide in Me, and My words abide in you, you will ask what you desire, and it shall be done for you. *By this My Father is glorified,* that you bear much fruit; so you will be My disciples" (John 15:7–8).

Prayer opens our hearts and minds to the ways of God

so that we know how to ask in His name…and He is glorified by bringing about the answers to our prayers.

For us to not have a significant prayer life is not only to deny ourselves the knowledge of God's will. It also means we'll be unable to obey and honor Him, and therefore, we'll be withholding from God the glory that's rightfully His.

MAY GOD BE GLORIFIED

In this book we've explored many aspects of Jesus' prayer life. Our prayer is that as you've read *Experiencing Prayer with Jesus* and looked at the Scriptures, the Spirit of God has stretched and challenged your life to desire a prayer life like Christ's, one that *brings glory to God* in the midst of a watching world.

Prayer continues to be the place where our wills are bent and submitted to the Father. It's the place where we find strength and understanding during difficult circumstances. It's in the place of prayer that we can cry out to the one who cannot only save us from death, but also give us life and meaning here and now. Prayer is the means for us to know the will of God so that knowing, we can obey Him and bring glory to Him before a watching world.

Now, in our day, we must take the example and teachings of Christ and faithfully apply them to our lives. The

Father's desire for each of us is to conform us to the image of His dear Son (Romans 8:29; see also Galatians 2:20). Have you released your life to God so He can shape your prayer life to mirror that of His Son?

Oh, that God would be glorified through us, through our individual prayer lives and the prayers of our families and churches! God's people desperately need "times of refreshing...from the presence of the Lord" (Acts 3:19), that revival might come to our nation and our world. God's people and a watching world must have a real and deep encounter with God and all of His fullness.

And when God's people return to Him in prayer—when they learn to pray as Jesus prayed—then we'll see the fulfillment of God's promise: "'Return to Me,' says the LORD of hosts, 'and I will return to you'" (Zechariah 1:3).

May we experience the prayer life of Jesus as He lives out His life in us (Galatians 2:20).

"It is written,

'My house is a house of prayer.'"

LUKE 19:46

YOUR PERSONAL RESPONSE:
ENCOUNTERING CHRIST
IN PRAYER

A Guide for Your Reflection
and Application

Use the questions, suggestions, and Scriptures in this section to deepen your commitment and progress toward a lifetime of experiencing prayer with Jesus.

You'll find this section to be helpful both individually as well as for small group study and discussion. Your sincere and prayerful answers in each section will go a long way in strengthening your experience of prayer in our Lord and Savior's presence.

RESPONDING TO THE INTRODUCTION: "FOR A LIFE-CHANGING ENCOUNTER WITH CHRIST"

- How would you describe your own desire and burden to grow in the area of prayer?

- What honest appraisal would you give of the present vitality and effectiveness of your prayers?
- What good reason do you have for *not* being discouraged about your prayer life in the future? (Remember to look to the Lord for this encouragement, and not to yourself.)
- Come before your Lord and Savior with the same request that His disciples made: "Teach me to pray." Acknowledge and thank Him as your Teacher, and ask Him to let *your* prayer life mirror the prayer experience of Jesus as revealed in the Scriptures.
- In light of your deepest desire for learning more about prayer from your Lord and Savior, make a new and stronger personal connection with His words of invitation in Matthew 11:28–30.

RESPONDING TO CHAPTER 1:
"OUR KEY TO LIFE AND MINISTRY"

- What impresses you most about our Savior's approach and commitment to prayer?
- When it comes to prayer, how much like the disciples are you in "wanting something better than they already had"?
- What convincing evidence do you see in Scripture that Jesus' prayer life was the key to both His life and ministry? What then does this say about the role prayer should play in *your* life?
- To what extent have you felt that praying as Christ

prayed is an unreasonable expectation for yourself and other Christians?

- Remember again that in Jesus' prayer life, we are seeing Christ "*in His humanity* praying to the Father, just as we pray to Him in our own humanity." What encouragement does this give you?

- Think of the particular weaknesses, failings, and weariness you've experienced in your prayer life. Then remember that *Christ understands.* He sympathizes with all those weaknesses, since He Himself has experienced temptation "in all points" as we have, yet without ever falling into sin (Hebrews 4:15). He understands all our temptations—and He's also our champion in triumphing over them. How does this truth help you? What does it show you not only about your need to follow in His steps, but also to actively depend upon His help?

- Bring quietly before God your answers to the questions included near the end of Chapter 1: "What can be said of your life—in the days of *your* flesh? Have you come to understand the importance of maintaining communication with God above everything else? What things have you let distract you from daily communication with the Father?"

- For the first disciples, the basic core of their calling from Christ was this: "that they might be with Him" (Mark 3:14). In what ways is that also *your* primary calling from the Lord?

RESPONDING TO CHAPTER 2:
"THE HEART OF OUR PRAYER"

- As you understand it, why was there so much emotion in the prayers of Jesus—so that He was described as praying "with vehement cries and tears" (Hebrews 5:7)?

- How well do you understand (as Jesus did) that everything the Father is doing in your life is out of a deep expression of His love?

- For Jesus, commitment to prayer sprang from a vital, loving relationship with the Father and the Father's loving presence in His life. Prayer was His lifeline. Why must this also be true for us?

- Bring quietly before God your sincere answers to these questions mentioned in Chapter 2:

  — "Are you experiencing intimate fellowship with the heavenly Father in the days of your flesh? Throughout each day, as you carry out your responsibilities and activities, are you living in continual fellowship with the Son and with the Father, through the Holy Spirit?"

  — "Have you, in prayer, allowed the Spirit to teach and shape you to the image of Christ so that you can say, 'If you've seen me, you've seen my heavenly Father' as Jesus did (John 14:9)? Have you spent enough time in prayer to know that your words and works are the words and works of the Father, as Jesus did (John 14:10)?"

  —"How deep is your relationship with the Lord as you pray? Do you pour your heart out to Him with complete confidence and trust in His help, because you've come to know and experience His love?"

- Knowing that a loving relationship with the Lord brings confidence into our prayer life—a confidence that leads to joy—how would you evaluate the degree of confidence and joy you experience in your prayers?
- Reflect on the opening words that Jesus taught us to say in prayer: "Our Father in heaven" (Luke 11:2). Think about all that this phrase means. What power and impact does it have personally for you?
- How do our prayers link heaven and earth together?

RESPONDING TO CHAPTER 3:
"OUR PURPOSE IN PRAYER"

- Jesus always approached prayer with a sense of divine accountability—a heart of reverent submission. Think about His example as you honestly answer these personal questions mentioned in Chapter 3:
  — "What's your heart attitude as you come to God in prayer? Do you find yourself arguing with the Lord when He brings an assignment? Does 'self' raise its head to rebel when you even hear that word *submit?*"
  — "Have you resolved that no matter what God reveals to you and requests of you through prayer, your answer is an unqualified *yes,* even before He shows you?"
- In what ways have you experienced the Lord communicating to you His clear direction and will as you've spent time with Him in prayer?
- As we observe and think about people's neediness all around us, how should we go about discerning God's

particular assignment for us in meeting those needs? In such a situation, what attitudes and requests should be present in our prayers?

- What will keep us from turning aside from the Lord's will for our lives?
- Have there been times when other people indicated to you that they "knew" God's will for your life? How did you respond?
- Here are more questions from Chapter 3 to carefully consider in regard to your life:

  — "Have you been willing to spend time in prayer at the front end of every assignment in order to gain God's perspective and instruction?"

  — "When was the last time you spent all night in prayer in order to receive the wisdom of God for your life?"

- In Gethsemane, Jesus clearly knew the load God was asking Him to carry. That load was indescribably difficult, and though He asked to be relieved of it, He also told His Father, "Not as I will, but as You will" (Matthew 26:39). Think about your Savior's example in Gethsemane as you review these questions from Chapter 3:

  — "Do you know what load God has for you to carry today?... Have you spent enough time with your Master to be instructed for His plans and purposes set aside for your life? In the midst of a hurting and troubled world, have you maintained a singleness of mind to hear your mission from God, just as Jesus did?"

- Specifically in your own life, what does it mean personally to pray for God's kingdom to come, and for His will to be done on earth as it is in heaven?
- What are you learning from the Lord Jesus about the most important things to pray for?

RESPONDING TO CHAPTER 4:
"RECEIVING GOD'S AGENDA"

- How should we prepare our hearts to release our own agenda in prayer, and to better receive God's agenda?
- What does it mean practically to be a good listener in prayer? What does that involve?
- What can we know for sure about the specific plans and purposes God has for each of our lives? And how can we go about discovering those plans and purposes?
- Review the following personal questions from Chapter 4. (Let them push you to deeper understanding of yourself and your prayer life.)

— "When you pray, are you on your own agenda, or listening to His? When was the last time you came to God in prayer, and even before you opened your mouth there was already an absolute, unconditional submission?"

— "What is God talking to you about when you pray? Not what are you talking to Him about, but what is He speaking with you about? What is the last thing God said to you when you went before Him in prayer?"

— "Are you communicating with the Lord to know without any question what He has purposed for you? Do you know the eternal significance of it all?"

— "Are you finding that He's opening your understanding as He comes alongside you to let you know what is on His agenda? Are you staying long enough in the Father's presence to allow Him to reveal to you His ways, truths, understanding, and agenda? Have you waited long enough before Him to know what it will cost you to carry out the assignment?"

- What helps you to realize that God's purposes are much larger than your own perspective on your current needs?
- Have you known times when an assignment from God has brought struggle and sorrow to your heart? If so, how freely were you able to share this burden with the Lord in prayer?
- What does it mean to you to "come to know the heart of God," as Chapter 4 discusses?
- How would you describe a healthy fear of God? What will that look like in your own heart and life?
- As you perceive it, what is on the heart of God for revival and spiritual awakening in your community, your country, and your world?
- Allow your heart to be connected in a new and stronger way to the words of Jesus in Matthew 9:37-38.

RESPONDING TO CHAPTER 5:
"OUR APPROACH IN PRAYER"

- How well have you done in setting aside and maintaining a regular time and place for prayer?
- How would you answer personally these questions from Chapter 5:
  — "What does your routine reveal about the importance of prayer in your life? Do people close to you know of your routines for prayer?"
  — "Have you established prayer in your life to such a degree that your spouse, your children, and your closest friends will know where and when to find you in prayer?"
- What can keep legalism from creeping into our habit of a regular time and place for prayer?
- What have you learned from the example of Jesus about the importance of *intensity* in prayer?
- Carefully consider your responses to these questions from Chapter 5:
  — "How would you describe the intensity of your own prayer life? Can you say that your petitions and supplication to the Father are marked by 'cries and tears'?"
  — "What do we have on our hearts when we come to pray as individuals and as churches? Have we become sidetracked or casual about our assignment as Christians, and in turn lost the passion of Christlike praying?"
- Why is it important to receive help from others, especially in prayer, in carrying our own load of following

the Lord? Do you have other believers in your life who
will help you do this?

- What does this prayer request mean to you: "Hallowed
  be Your name"?
- Chapter 5 states that "we must *think* both before we
  pray and while we pray." What kind of thinking is this?
  What does it actually involve?

RESPONDING TO CHAPTER 6:
"PRAYING FOR OTHERS"

- What are the most important things you've learned
  from the example of Jesus in praying for others?
- In the lives of those you pray for, what struggles are
  being faced? How is their faith being challenged at this
  time? How can you address these things in prayer?
- In His ministry to those around Him, Jesus depended
  on the Father's active guidance and direction through
  prayer for each step He took. Why was this so important for Him? And why is it important in your own
  ministry as well? What happens when we fail to depend
  on that step-by-step guidance as we minister to others?
- Consider your response to these questions from
  Chapter 6:
  — "To each of us, God has entrusted other people in a
  variety of relationships—a marriage partner, children,
  coworkers, friends, and a local church family.... Are you
  seeking the Father in prayer to understand His activity

in their lives? How much time in prayer have you spent on their behalf?"

— "As the Father reveals the people who have been entrusted to your life, are you faithfully going to God in intercession that they would remain faithful?"

— "How real, faithful, and intense is intercessory prayer in our lives? How much is being gained or lost in the lives of God's people through our praying?"

— "Are those around you being strengthened against sin and temptation because of your prayers?"

- What personal encouragement do you find from realizing that even now our Lord and Savior continues His ministry of intercession on our behalf?

- Remember that in the "Lord's Prayer," Jesus taught us to pray for *"our* daily bread" and to request forgiveness for *"our* sins." In practical terms, what does it mean to pray for others in this way?

- In regard to God's work in your family, your church, your community, your nation, and your world, what purposes of God and activities of God have been revealed to you?

- What do you learn from the example of Jesus about how to relate to those who oppose you? How can Christ's example help you when God places difficult people in your life?

RESPONDING TO CHAPTER 7:
"PRAYING FOR DAILY NEEDS"

- Take time immediately to offer thanksgiving and honor to God for His many gifts to you today in meeting your basic needs.
- How do you know for sure that God cares for your most basic needs? What gives you confidence about this?
- What are the most encouraging ways in which you've seen God's provision in your life?
- Why is forgiveness one of our daily needs?
- What is dangerous about failing to forgive others? How have you been made aware of this danger in your own life?
- Look with fresh eyes at the instruction we're given in Ephesians 4:32. How does this help you in regard to a life of experiencing forgiveness from the Lord and extending forgiveness to others?

RESPONDING TO CHAPTER 8:
"THE CERTAINTY OF GOD'S ANSWERS"

- What are the deepest reasons for the confidence Jesus had that His prayers on earth were being heard and answered by His Father in heaven?
- Reflect on these questions from Chapter 8:
  — "Have we cultivated a prayer life in which we can say along with Christ, 'Father, I know that You always hear me'?"

— "Have you consistently sought God in prayer believing that He hears and that He will reward your diligence to know Him?"

- Recall how the church in the Book of Acts was bold in seeking God through prayer in times of crisis. As a result, the Spirit's power was dynamically evident to them.

    — "What about our lives as Christians today? What about our churches? Have we followed the example of Christ and received God's answers and the Spirit's empowerment as a result?"

- In your own experience, in what instances have others around you failed to understand God's personal will for your life as He revealed it to you, and as you sought to live out His will?

- In Gethsemane, God the Father did not grant His Son's request for "the cup" to be removed. God's answer was no, but recall the resulting attitudes and actions of Jesus.

    — "How do *you* respond to God when His answer is no? When you make your request and God doesn't grant it, do you continue to argue with Him to try and get your way?"

- When you are seeking after God, how have you seen Him provide His strengthening provision for you in your times of particular weakness?

- How have you experienced God allowing you to understand and experience and appreciate His grace more fully when He does not grant something that you want and pray for? What does this teach you about His love and wisdom?

RESPONDING TO CHAPTER 9:
"PROTECTION FROM TEMPTATION"

- What is the key to our victory in temptation?
- What are the most important things you've learned from the example of Jesus in overcoming temptation?
- In your own life, what are the factors and circumstances that tend to make temptations harder to resist? How can prayer overcome this?
- For overcoming temptation, in what practical ways can you depend more fully on the resources of God?
- How often do you think about the Lord's full knowledge of the daily circumstances you face? How can an active awareness of this fact help you in prayer to prepare for everything you'll face each day?
- What answers would you give to these questions from Chapter 9:
  — "When you consider the struggles with temptation and sin in your own life, what role are you allowing prayer to play in this battle? How much time and energy are you willing to devote in prayer in order to receive victory over sin in your life?"
  — "Are you protecting yourself, your family, and your church from falling into temptation through active prayer to the Father?"

RESPONDING TO CHAPTER 10:
"OBEYING WHAT WE LEARN IN PRAYER"

- What have you learned about obedience from Jesus, your Lord and Savior?

- Even as a child, Jesus could say, "I must be about My Father's business" (Luke 2:49). In your own life, what application does that phrase have for you? What is the Father's business for you?

- Have you settled it in your heart that obedience to whatever God reveals to you in prayer is an absolute for you?

- In Chapter 10 we explore how Jesus, the Son of God, "learned obedience by the things which He suffered" (Hebrews 5:8). "It was precisely in His afflictions that Jesus 'learned' obedience in the sense of personally and practically taking hold of every aspect of obedience in every situation that awaited Him." How is that process also taking place in your own life?

- What has helped *you* to *grow* in obedience—to continue *learning* obedience, as Christ did?

- What can we learn from the example of Jesus about dependence on the Holy Spirit—and about our need for constant "intervention" and empowerment from the Spirit?

- How deep-rooted is your conviction that you absolutely cannot accomplish the Father's assignment in your life without the Spirit's active help and empowerment?
  — "If the Father has revealed His will and the manner in which He desires to use you, do you sense an urgent

need for the Father's 'intervention' on your behalf through the Spirit?"

— "Have you gone alone with God, as well as joined others in prayer, to receive 'power from on high' in order to gain strength, understanding, and direction to live out God's will?"

RESPONDING TO CHAPTER 11:
"GOD'S WILL ACCOMPLISHED"

- How free is the Father to fully accomplish His eternal purposes in your life? If you know of anything in your life which might be blocking this freedom, how can you remove this obstacle?

- In what ways is God using prayer to change and shape your life according to His redemptive will and purpose?

- In light of all you've learned about experiencing prayer with your Lord and Savior, make a new and stronger personal connection with His words in John 14:12–14. What "greater works" does He want to accomplish in your life as you make your requests in Jesus' name?
  — "In a day in which there is much prayer, are we therefore also seeing such 'greater works' as a result of those prayers?"

- What exactly is at stake through your prayer life?

- As you understand it, what kind of person does God use to change the course of history? How possible is it for *you* to be that kind of person?

- Are you fully convinced that God is in control and His ways are right? Is it therefore your heart's desire to immediately obey His direction as you discover it through deep, life-changing prayer?

RESPONDING TO CHAPTER 12:
"FOR THE GLORY OF GOD"

- What does the life of Jesus teach us about glorifying God?
- What does it mean to you to "be filled with all the fullness of God" (Ephesians 3:19)?
- How exactly is God being glorified through His answers to your prayers?

CONCLUSION

This book's introduction mentions five goals from the authors, and they're listed again below for your reflection. What has God been doing in your heart in regard to each one of them?

"1. To open afresh your mind and heart to the prayer life of Jesus.

"2. To help you anticipate and recognize the activity of God in your prayer life as He conforms you to the image of His Son.

"3. To exhort you to obey and respond to all of the fullness of God—Father, Son, and Holy Spirit—as He develops your prayer life.

"4. To help you see the immediate urgency of the hour in which we live, and the impact we can have through our prayers.

"5. To show that immediate and thorough obedience is key to your prayer life."

As you reflect on how these goals are being accomplished in your own life, give thanks to God for all that He has done and is doing in bringing you into closer fellowship with our Lord.

About the Authors

 Dr. Henry Blackaby, president of Blackaby Ministries International, is the author of more than a dozen books, including the classic *Experiencing God* and the recently released *Experiencing the Cross*. He earned his B.D. and Th.M. from Golden Gate Seminary and holds four honorary doctorate degrees. Dr. Blackaby has spent his life in ministry, serving as a church planter, pastor, and missionary. Today, his primary message is an urgent call for spiritual leadership and revival across North America and around the world. Henry and his wife, Marilynn, have five children, all of whom are actively serving in full-time Christian ministry. They also have fourteen grandchildren. They make their home in Atlanta, Georgia.

Dr. Norman C. Blackaby serves as vice president of Blackaby Ministries International, where his responsibilities include preaching, leading conferences, and directing the online training center. He and his father coauthored *Called and Accountable: Discovering Your Place in God's Eternal Purpose*. Prior to joining Blackaby Ministries, Norman served in Texas as a senior pastor. He holds a Ph.D. in biblical backgrounds and has taught at two seminaries in the fields of backgrounds and spiritual development. He currently resides in Cochrane, Alberta, with his wife, Dana, and their three children, Emily, Douglas, and Anne.

About Blackaby Ministries International

Blackaby Ministries International was established to respond to increasing opportunities for ministry globally. The heart-cry of the Blackaby family is to disciple God's people in such a way that God's Holy Spirit would bring revival in the hearts of God's people and spiritual awakening to a lost world.

The key components of Blackaby Ministries International include marketplace ministry, articles and books, training institutes, international conferences, and preaching, teaching, and speaking. The ministry's website is www.blackaby.org.

For further information:

Blackaby Ministries International
P.O. Box 16338
Atlanta, GA 30321
e-mail: information@blackaby.org

SCRIPTURE INDEX

2005 NATIONAL DAY OF PRAYER THEME BOOK
FROM MAX LUCADO

TURN
Remembering Our Foundations
MAX LUCADO ISBN 1-59052-450-0

The very breath that sustains you. The prosperity of our land. Both—
and everything in between—are gifts from the same God. Remember
Him. And *turn* to Him in heartfelt prayer.

ჯ Dare to Go There ჯ

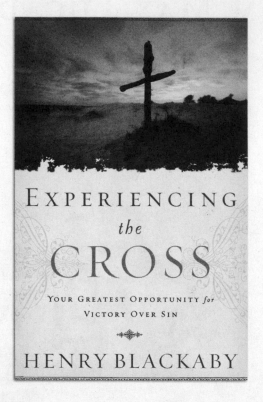

Although the cross is God's decisive deed in human history, the full meaning of it is far too much for a mere human mind to grasp. But through Henry Blackaby's careful examination, the cross becomes not a doctrine, but an experience. Steeped in the Blackaby distinctive of constant encouragement toward your personal experience of God and firmly rooted in Scripture, this book exposes the tragic result of a casual attitude toward the sin in our lives that made the cross necessary. Learn to surrender to the deeper dimensions of the cross so that nothing can block the Lord's presence and power in your life!

ISBN 1-59052-480-2 • Book
ISBN 1-59052-599-X • Study Guide

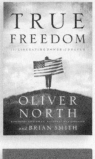

True Freedom
The Liberating Power of Prayer
OLIVER NORTH & BRIAN SMITH ISBN 1-59052-363-6

Honorary National Day of Prayer chairman Oliver North illustrates the freeing effects of prayer through engaging stories and scriptural truths.

RIGHT WITH GOD
Loving Instruction from the Father's Heart
RON MEHL ISBN 1-59052-186-2

Christianity's best-known Scripture is not a series of ominous warnings, but the greatest statement of God's love. Award-winning author Ron Mehl provides a unique interpretation of the Ten Commandments.

CERTAIN PEACE IN UNCERTAIN TIMES
Embracing Prayer in an Anxious Age
SHIRLEY DOBSON ISBN 1-57673-937-6

Respond to change in a chaotic world with inner peace and resolve. National Day of Prayer Task Force chairperson Shirley Dobson shows you how to nurture an efffective and lasting lifestyle of prayer.

THE PRAYER OF JABEZ, 5TH ANNIVERSARY EDITION
Breaking Through to the Blessed Life
BRUCE WILKINSON ISBN 1-59052-475-6

Are you ready to reach for the extraordinary? Join Bruce Wilkinson to discover how the remarkable prayer of a little-known Bible hero can release God's favor, power, and protection.

CROSSINGS®
THE BOOK CLUB FOR TODAY'S CHRISTIAN FAMILY

A Letter to Our Readers

Dear Reader:
In order that we might better contribute to your reading enjoyment, we would appreciate your taking a few minutes to respond to the following questions. When completed, please return to the following:

Andrea Doering, Editor-in-Chief
Crossings Book Club
401 Franklin Avenue, Garden City, NY 11530

You can post your review online! Go to www.crossings.com and rate this book.

Title _____ Author _____

1 Did you enjoy reading this book?

❑ Very much. I would like to see more books by this author!

❑ I really liked_____

❑ Moderately. I would have enjoyed it more if_____

2 What influenced your decision to purchase this book? Check all that apply.

    ❑ Cover
    ❑ Title
    ❑ Publicity
    ❑ Catalog description
    ❑ Friends
    ❑ Enjoyed other books by this author
    ❑ Other _____

3 Please check your age range:

    ❑ Under 18   ❑ 18-24
    ❑ 25-34   ❑ 35-45
    ❑ 46-55   ❑ Over 55

4 How many hours per week do you read? _____

5 How would you rate this book, on a scale from 1 (poor) to 5 (superior)?
_____

Name_____

Occupation_____

Address_____

City_____ State_____ Zip_____